6·12·86

ADVENTURES WITH LIQUEURS

Adventures
with
Liqueurs

"A shared experience"

by

Lucienne M.L. De Wulf   Marie-Françoise Fourestier

BOOKS IN
FOCUS Inc.
bringing you
books that matter

Manufactured in the United States of America

Library of Congress Catalog Card Number 78-74589

ISBN 0-916728-14-5

Books In Focus, Inc.
Suite 31B
160 East 38th Street
New York, N.Y. 10016

Telephone: (212) 490-0334

Typography: Steve Elmaleh

Cover Illustration: *Pousse-Café,* courtesy of
MARIE BRIZARD LIQUEURS (Schieffelin & Co.)

TABLE OF CONTENTS

PART III A Voyage Through
the World of Liqueurs

INTRODUCTION

AN INVITATION

Welcome to the exciting world of Liqueurs! You are about to begin an adventurous journey which will stimulate both your imagination and palate; a journey which will add a new dimension of flavor to your drinking and dining pleasure.

Adventures With Liqueurs tells you all about the fascinating history and development of liqueurs, and does more. The Authors show you exactly how to enjoy liqueurs in many diverse and interesting ways - as apéritifs, in cooking and desserts and appetizers, after dinner cordials and much more. There are enough suggestions and recipes to keep you and your acquaintances experiencing new liqueur delights for years to come! Delights which will add a new dimension to your lifestyle and enhance your shared experiences.

For centuries, liqueurs have been valued as elixirs, potions, curatives, and even as aphrodisiacs. You are now invited to enter the world of liqueurs, and to enjoy its exquisite pleasures!

PART I
WHERE LIQUEURS COME FROM: THEIR HISTORY AND DEVELOPMENT

The history of liqueurs is closely linked to the history of ancient alcoholic beverages. The most common were some form of wine made from grapes, dates or rice, and beer.

We don't know how men discovered fermented beverages, it may have been pure chance, but they were quick to recognize the benefits and delights of those "nectars". Since then, men have searched for different ways to create new, strong alcoholic beverages that would give them a euphoric feeling and taste good as well.

Fermentation was already known in the Neolithic period, which preceded the first historical civilization, that of Sumer. Sumer was located in the Persian Gulf between two rivers, the Tigris and the Euphrates, where today Saudi Arabia, Iraq and Iran meet. Because this was a particularly fertile area in barley and wheat, the Sumerians used almost half of their harvest in the making of beer. Brewers were usually women and they sold the beer from their homes. Later, when the popularity of fermented drinks increased, it was sold from taverns in such quantity that Hammurabi, one of the great rulers of Mesopotamia, was impelled to warn people against poor quality and high-priced beer, found in public places.

Beer was consumed not only for pleasure but was also used by doctors to treat their patients. Some of their known remedies, prepared from crushed snake skins, turtle scales and herbs such as thyme and cassia, were powdered and mixed with beer. Beer helped hide the bad taste of the mixture and speeded the "effectiveness" of the remedy.

In the area which harbored three great civilizations—the Sumerian, Mesopotamian and Egyptian, the most plentiful ingredients were barley, wheat, dates, figs and honey.

In Mesopotamia, the successors of the Sumerians drank beer, but later, when the soil stopped yielding such plentiful crops they had to turn to date wines, the most popular fermented juice of antiquity.

In Egypt the poor drank beer, the rich drank date wines and the priests who thought that the vines were a gift from the Gods, used only grape wines in their rituals. They attributed the vine to Osiris, the god of nature who was worshiped when the Nile

1

overflowed once a year and fertilized the plain. The inundations were celebrated by ritual festivals where a great deal of wine was drunk by the priests. This is why Osiris became known as the lord of the wines.

Whatever their origin, these wines were not what they are today. Often they were aromatized with herbs, spices and fruits. They were very sweet,of a thick consistency, and the Egyptians drank them mixed with water. Their favorite herbs were fennel, absinthe and saffron. Rose petal water and fennel was a popular drink of Babylon. In Ancient Greece, a common practice was to make a cordial with honey and herbs, called Hydromel. Mead, once the favorite beverage of Viking and Germanic tribes in England, and now regaining popularity, is derived from the Hydromel recipe.

The practice of mixing wine with herbs and spices spread all over the Mediterranean with the help of the Phoenicians. They were the great travelers and skilled sailors of the time, dominating the Mediterranean commerce of aromatic herbs and spices. To protect their monopoly, they invented horrifying stories about the countries they visited.

Date wine was familiar to Greece but because of this exchange and commerce and the abundance of grapes in Greece, grape wine became the dominant drink. This is why Dionysus is said to have left Mesopotamia, a beer-drinking country, for Greece!

Dionysus was the son of Zeus and Semele. Hera, jealous of Semele when she became the object of her husband's affection, perfidiously suggested that Semele ask her lover to show himself to her in all his splendor. Zeus reluctantly agreed, and Semele was killed by a thunderbolt. However, Zeus seized the child from its mother's body, stitched it into his thigh and at the right time the infant emerged perfectly formed. The young Dionysus, or twice-born as he was known, was brought up by the nymphs of Mount Nysa in Upper Armenia. It was in the countryside surrounding Mount Nysa that Dionysus discovered the vine and its uses. In the form of a man, he began to teach mortals how to cultivate the vine and how to worship it through its god. Thus, the Dionysiac cult was developed and its festivals placed under the sign of Fecundity, symbolized by the vine. Even the Greek Gods, on Mount Olympus, indulged in Dionysus' gift.

Two traditions are mixed in this mythical figure: the first and earlier one made Dionysus a divinity of plants, fruits and foliage. The second which made him the god of fertility and fecundity quickly underwent several revisions deeming him the divinity of the vineyard and of wine, and by extension, the patron of music, dance and of the arts in general.

In classical Greece, the art of wine-making was perfected and the expensive wines from Lesbos and Chios were enjoyed among the upper class. Still, this wine bore very little resemblance to contemporary wine because the Greeks kept the Egyptian custom of diluting wine with water. The finer wines were often as thick as honey. Fermentation

2

was not very scientific and ancient wines spoiled rapidly unless special ingredients were added such as a concoction of herbs and spices. Each region had its own secret ways.

As good as the Greek wines were, the Italian wines were even better. Ancient Rome was the crossroad of western culture; it not only inherited Greek culture but also became acquainted through its conquests with the East and the North. The Romans kept the custom of adding plants, herbs and spices to wine and used the result extensively in cooking and medicine. They recognized that some plants had cleansing as well as medicinal qualities. Lavender and mint were used to perfume their bath. Their favorite ingredients were cinnamon, ginger, myrrh and cardomon.

The tradition of making aromatizing wines, both for pleasure and medicinal purposes, continued through the centuries with few changes until the invention of the distillation apparatus, the alembic, and the consequent understanding of the process itself. The making of spirits is commonly associated with alchemists during the late Middle Ages, though alchemy has a much more ancient origin.

The idea of transmuting base metals into noble ones probably originated in the Greek colony of Alexandria in the early part of the Christian era. The notion was transmitted to Western Europe by the Arabs when they conquered Spain. Numerous legends surround the origin of alchemy. According to one study it was founded by the Egyptian God Toth (Hermes) who invented arts and science and was the master of those interested in nature. This is why later alchemists called their work, the "hermetic art." They put the seal of Hermes upon their vessels, hence the origin of the phrase "hermetically sealed". Another story attributes the origin of alchemy to the fallen angels mentioned in the book of Genesis. These wicked creatures bestowed their wives with only a limited knowledge of the properties of gold, silver, precious stones and herbs. Another legend claims that alchemy was revealed by God to Moses and Aaron. All of this is very picturesque but it is more likely that alchemy originated in the Greek colony of Alexandria. This was probable since a preoccupation with the idea of transmutation of matter was prominent in classical Greek writings. The search for easy gold was not their only pursuit. Alchemists were the forerunners of modern chemists.

With the discovery of alcohol by the Arabs and the invention of the alembic the alchemists began to experiment with this magnificent liquid. At first, they thought they had discovered a universal panacea—aqua vitae—the water of life. And indeed it was a potent medicine and seemed to prolong life.

The work of the alchemist in these superstitious times was tinged with accusations and with rumors of magic and sorcery. The paintings of the time always portrayed the alchemist as an old man surrounded by a myriad of tubes and fumes; it was easy for the uninitiated to look upon the alchemists as being associated with the devil.

Distillation gained some respectability when it was perfected by the medical schools of Salerno (Italy) and Montpellier (France) in the eleventh and twelfth centuries. Their teachings were essentially based on translations into Latin of Arabic medical works. The Arabs were innovators in all domains and were authorities on pharmacy and hygiene. Wherever they went they brought their favorite luxuries, such as roses, oranges and sugar cane with them.

Salerno contributed to the proliferation of elixirs, potions, and tonics, by making the first truly scientific distillation. They succeeded in obtaining a purer alcohol. However, crude results of distillation were so abominable-tasting, so unfit for any civilized palate, that herbs, fruits and spices had to be added to mask the taste of it and give it some color.

Contributing to the early popularity of liqueurs was the importance of monasteries in France. Living in a self-enclosed world, Monks had to know how to survive from their environment alone. Since it was their duty to take care of the sick on their lands, they were keenly aware of the medicinal values of plants and they installed alembics in convents as soon as they were known. The Church frowned on these activities for moral reasons since the difference between love potions, witchcraft and medieval beverages was not clear-cut. The competitors, would-be doctors and apothecaries, considered them as formidable opponents since people were more inclined to trust a remedy made by a monk.

Monasteries were located in the countryside. Monks, having both leisure time and space started herb gardens to cultivate exotic plants not grown in their area. These plants were brought into France by returning crusaders, travelers, peddlers and pilgrims. Finally, for convenience—to have them at their finger tips, and to save themselves long walks into the countryside, the monks added local herbs to their gardens. Among the herbs that became staples of an herb garden were:

Lily: for calming the love fires

Sage: for keeping healthy, to improve memory, against declining faculties—the plant of longevity and of memory

Rue: the Romans thought it good for the eyes and hence it became known as giving second sight. They considered it also a symbol of chastity: it was the herb given by Mercury to Ulysses to overcome Circe's charm, and used as an antidote for her love potion. In the Middle Ages it became a powerful anti-plague remedy. It is said that thieves used to drink a potion with rue to escape capture while robbing plague-infested houses and villages.

Rose: rose water has been used extensively for perfumes and for remedies

4

La cave de vieillissement. The aging cellar of the Carthusian Monastery in Voiron, France.

5

VUE DU MONASTERE DE LA GRANDE CHARTREUSE.

18th century view of the mother house of the order in the Dauphine, the Alps.

Aconit: a partly poisonous plant also known as the Monk's-hood or the Wolf's-bane because it was used to fight off the numerous wolves of the time. The root helped to control fever and bring down high blood pressure. The legend goes that Hercules fought with Cerberus, the many-headed dog who guarded the gates of the Underworld on a hill named Aconitus. The fight was terrible and Cerberus was foaming at the mouth. From this foam sprang a venomous plant they called aconit.

Watercress: known to be good for brain damage and to cure toothaches.

In each monastery, there was at least one monk in charge of preserving and keeping herbs, and one monk who was a doctor. Competing with monasteries were the Royal gardens. Since kings lived in terror of being poisoned, they wanted to have their own garden so that their private doctors could take care of them.

It was only much later that the "Jardin des Simples" became the botanical garden—a place to display and grow exotic plants, trees or flowers.

Another important factor in the development and rise of liqueurs was the Great Plague which raged through Europe from 1348 to 1352. The combination of alcohol and plants was supposed to be an antiseptic, and the euphoria brought about by alcohol prevented people from being overcome by the tragic reality. One doesn't know what was worse: the disease itself or the fear of it.

The consumption of liqueurs rose sharply and the gardens grew to answer this demand. The distillation process became more sophisticated. The monks couldn't supply all the demands and the apothecaries began to have a greater share of the markets and were finally recognized as useful and official members of society.

The population at large began to enjoy the taste of liqueurs so much that some enthusiasts became addicts and steps had to be taken by the government and the church to limit its use.

It was about this time that the accounts of Marco Polo's voyage became known and with them interesting insights into the nature of drinking habits in faraway lands. In Persia for example, there grew beautiful grapes from which delicious wines were made. Though the Muslims don't drink wine, they got around this interdiction by boiling the wine and declaring that once boiled it wasn't wine anymore. But in Ispahan, date wine with spices were prevalent. The first time that one drank the wine it had a very strong purgative effect, but one very soon became accustomed to it.

In the Gaindu province near Tibet, wine was made from wheat and rice and multiple spices which were abundant in that area and unkown in the west: cloves, ginger and cinamon.

In Catai (China) there were no grapes but the natives made a rice wine with spices "that was better than any other wine." It was clear, sparkling and fragrant but since it was hot, very hot, and very sweet, the unsuspecting traveler would get terribly drunk even after a few glasses.

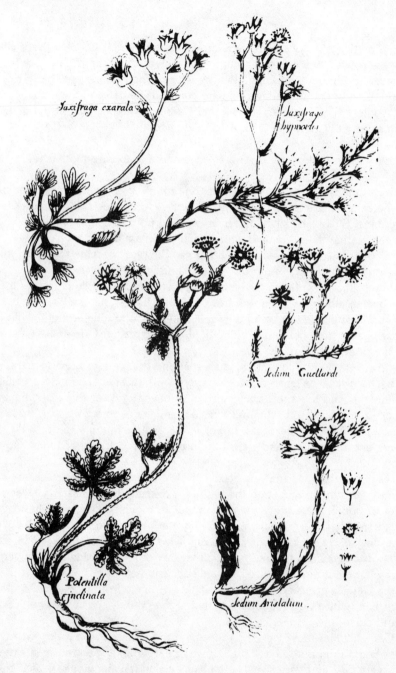

Saxifraga exarata

Saxifraga hypnoides

Sedum Guettardi

Potentilla crinata

Sedum Aristatum

Flore du Dauphiné — 18ème siècle. (1) Alpine flowers of the 18th century.

8

In the city of Quinsai, "the City of Heaven", in China, there were no grapes or grape wines. Delicious dried grapes and wines were imported but nobody liked them. They preferred the traditional rice and spice wines. It was called the City of Heaven, not because of its wine but because of its charming, unforgettable courtesans who could give their customers an idea of paradise.

In Sumatra, there was no grape wine, no rice wine and no date wine, but there was an extraordinary tree. If you cut the branches of this tree, wine would flow out red or white according to the type of tree. Day and night the natives kept pots under the cut branches. This beverage tasted very good and could cure water retention, coughing, and melancholia. When the wine stopped flowing, according to legend, they would water the tree and a few hours later it would start all over again.

This extraordinary tree was also found in India in the province of Malabar. A Christian colony settled here whose mission was to guard the tomb of St. Thomas, the Apostle. They not only had these extraordinary trees but also the "Noix du Pharaon" (coconut trees). Marco Polo was very struck by this useful fruit of which no part was wasted. Its fibers made clothes; one ate the flesh and drank the juice—"a meal and a suit in one fruit!"

But in Rosie (Russia) they drank a very "perfect" wine called Cervoise, which was actually closer to beer than to wine. Quite often, men, women, and children would sit in the taverns and consume large quantities of Cervoise. The innkeeper would keep track of everybody's tab and at the end of the day accounts would be settled. If a man ran out of money he would borrow some on the head of one of his children and eventually sell the child to a foreign merchant. Indeed it must have been a "perfect" wine.

Little did the Venetian explorer know when he was dictating his memoirs out of boredom, in a Genovese prison in 1280, that a century later his book would be read with passion and enthusiasm by a wide public and a new generation of travelers; Vasco de Gama and Christopher Columbus. Until then, there was only one route to the East which was entirely controlled by the Muslim world and had been closed to Western traders. Why share a profit? Marco Polo helped these European adventurers discover new horizons and taught them that there was more than one road leading to spices and silks. He inspired the Italians, the Spanish, the Portuguese, the Dutch and the English, all of seafaring countries, to further explore the world.

Some similarities between the early cordials and the liqueurs we enjoy today began developing after Columbus' great journey to the New World and the English and Dutch expeditions to China.

New ingredients such as sugar cane, cinnamon, mace, nutmeg, quinquina, vanilla and pineapple played an important part in their increasing popularity. Liqueurs began to taste better and to be enjoyed for themselves.

The spice trade had other consequences besides improving the quality of liqueurs. Once the first step was taken, spices became the greatest item of international commerce, open to all. Whatever changes occured in the political spheres, nothing stopped the steady flow of the spice trade.

This commerce was responsible for closer relations between nations. It brought the East and the West into permanent contact with each other. After the year 1500 one cannot separate the history of commerce and navigation from the history of spices. When Bartholomew Diaz discovered the most southern point of Africa, the Cape of Good Hope, in 1487, he probably wasn't aware that he was opening up a new historical era.

Today, we look at cloves[1], mace, nutmeg, pepper[2], and cinnamon as pleasant commodities. In those times they were a sure road to wealth. The quest for spices led to bitter quarrels and endless wars between the exploring nations. In 1750 they used to say that "No lover ever guarded his beloved more jealously than did the Dutch, the Island of Amboina (Maluccas) where the clove trees grow." A Frenchman, Pierre Le Poivre, managed to steal not pepper, but nutmeg and clove trees from the Dutch, spreading these spices all over the world.

The Renaissance was a time of endless marvels and discoveries, and it also brought to France, as the King's bride, a demure italian girl, Catherine de Medicis. She altered not only the course of French history but also the drinking and eating habits of her adopted country. She was fond of good food, drink and liqueurs and she brought along from Italy, her own chefs and liqueur makers because the French were not, at the time, up to Italian standards. This created a healthy competitive feeling which led to continuous improvement, new varieties and new tastes. Drinking liqueurs became fashionable at court and among the elegant circles of the upper class.

Catherine certainly refined French cooking. A description of a dinner in her times makes you wonder what French cooking must have been like before:

> …four hours at the table….sixty-five courses….each course
> consisting of three different dishes….served on the finest
> silver….choirs and harpsichords and lutes….

It is not surprising that liqueurs began then to be used as digestives: Most liqueurs contained herbs or plants known for their digestive qualities; and the letter *D* for digestive still stands today in France on some liqueur labels. The indulgence in gargantuan meals took a long time to disappear. It is enough to read the description of a Victorian supper to understand why tightly corseted ladies were strongly in need of a digestive. The liqueur helped them to survive until they could retire and take off their "armor".

---

[1] The name of this nail-shaped spice is derived from the French word "clou". The Chinese used to chew it to sweeten their breath and if you put it in a pan of water on your radiator, it will deodorize your room.

[2] Cayenne pepper (red) is useful as a stimulant. It gives tone to the circulation and in winter it will warm your feet if you sprinkle a little of it in the bottom of your socks.

Catherine de Medicis also brought the tablecloth, the fork, ice cream and her own alchemists to France, not to make gold, but to take care of her personal health which also meant the dispatch of her greatest and most dangerous enemies to the next world. On your next trip to France, visit the Castle of Blois, and see the room where her alchemists prepared gloves, flowers, rings and all sorts of deadly gifts.

Dealing with esoteric beverages was a common practice in every social class. In a world full of cruelty and inexplicable phenomena, everybody from the courtiers to the peasants, turned to religion and superstition for comfort. They often visited fortune tellers and witches who offered a cure for every ill and the fulfillment of every dream: magic philters, tonics, remedies for unwanted pregnancies and means to hasten inheritances. Love potions and aphrodisiacs were the most in demand, and had names such as Oil of Venus, Lover's Delight, Perfect Love and Total Felicity. Their use is a very ancient one. Tristan and Isolde would not have become such passionate lovers without the philter they were given by mistake. This practice persisted into the 17th century and climaxed in the famous "Affaire des Poisons" which compromised the flower of the French aristocracy. Mme de Montespan, one of the mistresses of the Sun King, used to visit witches and have black masses said in the hope that these practices would help her keep the King's love. She was accused of trying to poison him when she really only fed him numerous aphrodisiacs. The miracle is that they did not kill him. This scandal led to the burning of several witches.

The authorities, aware of the growing abuses, enacted stricter and stricter regulations for the manufacturing of liqueurs, cordials and tonics. The "professional" liqueur makers wanted to protect themselves from false accusations and dangerous imitations that would taint their reputation . They created a union of distillers, and to this day liqueur manufacturers have to follow strict government standards.

In the 18th century the new regulations made people less suspicious of liqueurs. The special ingredients arriving into the country from the East and the West contributed even more to their desire for experimentation with new tastes. Plants brought in from the East were experimented with in the ever-enlarging gardens of the rich and the kings. Little by little the gardens stopped being devoted only to medicinal purposes and by the 18th century, they became showcases for rare flowers and trees. It was then that botany became a science which led to more and more sophisticated gardens and finally to what we now call botanical gardens

This was also the time when Marie Brizard began using anise seed as a universal panacea and created the famous liqueur, anisette. When the ancestors of creme de cacao, creme de menthe and curaçao appeared on the market, they reached a wider and wider audience through the opening of public coffee houses which soon stopped serving only coffee. In cafes, an almost exclusively male clientele would gather to savor the sweet and colorful liqueurs, to discuss politics, philosophy and to play chess.

The French Revolution put a stop to all these mundane activities. The country was in a turmoil, heads were falling by the thousands. France was attacked by the whole of Europe. The monasteries were destroyed and closed and the monks dispersed. The recipes for monastic liqueurs such as Chartreuse and Benedictine, to cite only two, were lost. It is likely that only the purely medicinal potions were still used and that the more sophisticated luxury liqueurs suffered.

When order prevailed again, under Napoleon, distillers, scientists and inventors were able to resume their activities and experimentations in peace. One of the most important discoveries at the beginning of the 19th century was the process of rectification which led to a purer alcohol and better liqueurs. At the same time international trade was booming, bringing with it new raw materials, new markets and new products.

By the end of the 19th century, the great cordial houses were solidly established: Bols and De Kuyper in Holland, Stock in Italy, Cusenier, Cointreau and Grand Marnier in France.

As far as liqueurs are concerned, the 20th century has brought new scientific progress which simplified the process, helped render liqueur-making easier, but has certainly not brought about any drastic change in the traditional methods. Only natural ingredients are used (fruits, herbs, plants, peels, spices and essences) and the base remains a high quality alcohol. The secret of the formulas are as well kept as they were in the medieval times.

Technological advances have helped bring the price of liqueurs down; today, they are available not only to royalty, aristocracy and the rich, but most importantly, to all who recognize and appreciate quality and fine taste.

PART II

WHAT ARE LIQUEURS AND CORDIALS AND HOW ARE THEY MADE?

The Heart of The Matter: Cordials or Liqueurs?

Should these "marvels" of man's ingenuity be called cordials or liqueurs? Indeed, the two words—cordials and liqueurs—have become synonymous. It is sometimes implied that cordials are "types", such as crème de menthe, curaçao or anisette, and that liqueurs are one of a kind. But they both describe the same sweet and powerful drink and they are both defined by law as a "sweetened liquor with a proof of 40% or more." If in Europe the term liqueur seems to have taken over, in the U.S.A. both are used. The choice is yours.

The word *cordial* comes from the Latin "cor" meaning the heart. The basic connotation of the word implies that cordials had some *curative* value. They were prescribed by doctors to bring comfort to the heart; they were and still are "heart-warming." In medieval times cordial spirits were referred to as *Vital Spirits*, for the vital spirits reside in the heart. It is not amazing that words such as *cardiac, core, courage,* to mention a few, have the same origin, and that to "be cordial" is to be warm, stimulating and cheering: a social delight.

On the other hand, the word *liqueur* is a more recent acquisition. It also comes from the Latin. *Liquor* means clear and liquid, similar to water but with the understanding that it has a strong alcoholic content. It describes a beverage that is sweetened and softened with aromatics. In today's language the two terms, cordial and liqueur, are interchangeable, one acquiring the dimension of the other.

The End Result of a Glorious Blending; What are Liqueurs and Cordials?

Whether in Europe, the U.S., or any other part of the world, a product must fulfill three conditions to be considered a liqueur. It must (1) have a spirit base, (2) be flavored, and (3) be sweetened. The choice and proportions of the three basic elements vary according to countries, manufacturers, individual formulas and of course the availability of the raw materials. The possible combinations are infinite and this accounts for an endless variety of liqueurs.

Liqueur, a glorious title that implies responsibility, is the harmonious blending of several ingredients whose equilibrium is essential for the development of its unique character, the richness of its flavor and the fullness of its aroma. The blend includes:

1. Its base; carefully selected quality brandies and spirits.
2. Its lacing; a golden syrup made from honey or sugar.
3. Its true identity; natural flavoring from aromatic substances of vegetal origin such as flowers, fruits, peels, berries, barks, herbs, seeds, roots and spices; alone or in any combination.

This "harmonious blending" shows us why liqueurs have been adopted since the beginning of time as medicinal remedies, love potions, aphrodisiacs and of course, as secret elixirs, and it also determines the different methods of production that can be used in creating a liqueur.

It all appears simple but this "perfect" measuring and balancing is the result of human experience and as such is achieved through the tedious process of trial and error. Each success was, and still is, preserved for posterity in closely guarded secret formulas. In an ever modern and technical society this reestablishes the value of tradition and long term experience alongside the newest technological discoveries. The manufacturing process is comparable in complexity to the making of wines or spirits. The standards are very high. The end product is an object of art with a perfect taste, a beautiful fragrance and an extraordinary color.

16

Ingredients From Around The World; The Perfect Beginning

In the "How to Succeed Book" about liqueurs, the first principle is to preserve the flavor, the aroma and all the essential qualities of the natural ingredient whether it is a flower, a seed, or any other aromatic substance. One must achieve this goal throughout the several stages needed to perfect this work of art; by adhering to the condition prescribed in the formula, and by carrying them out in their prescribed order.

Distillation and blending require the utmost care. The object is not only to preserve, but also to prevent any other "taste or fragrance or qualities" from interfering with the essential qualities of the basic ingredient.

Standards of taste and quality required for a particular liqueur are established. The choice of aromatic substances and the amounts of ingredients in specific formulae often go back to XVth or XVIth century manuscripts. The master blender may have to readjust the formula to meet the standards implied or understood in it. Precise decision making is the most important factor in the final testing.

Favorite beverages are often made from the products plentiful in a particular region. It is interesting to note that most XIXth century European liqueur houses were established in areas where fruits, herbs or spices were readily available. Fruits came from the Loire, Garonne or Rhone valleys in France and the valley of the Po in Italy. Herbs grew in the mountainous regions throughout Europe and on the sea-cliffs of the Atlantic or Mediterranean, to cite only a few places. Most of the valleys of the world were destined to become world-famous cordial centers.

The art of the liqueur maker starts with a careful selection of the fruits, plants, seeds, and flowers needed to aromatize the liqueur. These are not easy to handle and several important factors must be considered when selecting the right ingredient. It has been known, since antiquity, that to make a successful liqueur with plants, one has to pick the plant in good weather, sometimes at high altitudes. Advice, good or bad, has always been given to those who wanted to use aromatic plants to flavor food and drink.

The first factor to keep in mind is the place of origin of the ingredient. Liqueurs used to be made with regional herbs or fruits. It was a way of preserving abundant crops and utilizing the "fruits of the earth" most efficiently. Some plants were important and essential even to the concocting of medicines and great use was made of those that were grown locally. The soil and climate are important factors in the quality of fruits. Their flavor, water and sugar content will be higher or lower depending on whether the year has been rainy, dry, sunny, cloudy, hot or cold. Crops can be a success or a failure in both quantity or quality. Groves, orchards and fields are being developed in countries or regions where there is a minimum chance of soil and climatic variations.

Harvesting is so important that whole crops can be destroyed if the timing is off. The Druids in Gaul and in the British Isles picked their plants according to a very strict and complicated ritual. Vervain, a plant still used today in many herb liqueurs and the basic ingredient of the Vervaine de Velay, was gathered on certain specific days: at the beginning of the dog days (from early July to early September). The priests were not to be seen either by the sun or the moon. Plants are so delicate to gather and to keep that one should only harvest what one needs. They should be picked when dry, handled with care and gathered separately so as not to adulterate their perfumes or qualities.

It is not surprising that inside old apothecaries' shops, there were rows and rows of dark small wooden drawers, just as in the dark, cool, dry plant room of a monastery.

Fruits have to picked as closely as possible to the time of their maturity since they reach their full flavor and greatest fragrance then. They are very perishable, very delicate and very seasonal. They should be processed immediately after their harvest. If one deals with mature fruit, which is the best, maceration on the spot makes it possible to catch the fruit at its prime.

Roots are at their best in autumn; flowers when they are first fully opened and still contain all of their essential oils; seeds when completely mature.

Once the harvest is completed, it is important either to process "the fruits of the earth" immediately or to take steps to preserve them in the most efficient and appropriate way. The object is to retain both flavor and fragrance of the harvested crop until it can be incorporated into the liqueurs.

The preservation of the ingredients has to be made under certain conditions to retain flavor and aroma. Very specific advice has been given since ancients times on how to preserve the perfumes and virtues of the plants. These were used not only in beverages but also in perfumes, for cooking, coloring or as medicines.

Drying the fruits is necessary when they do not travel well or when they cannot be processed immediately. This process is also used for certain fruits whose concentrated flavor is needed to meet the demands of the formula. When modern transportation was not available, certain formulas were created using the dried fruits. Such is the case for orange peels. They had to travel a long way and had to be preserved. When fresh fruits are used the formula is adjusted. The basic taste of fresh fruit is different from the concentrated flavor of the dried fruit.

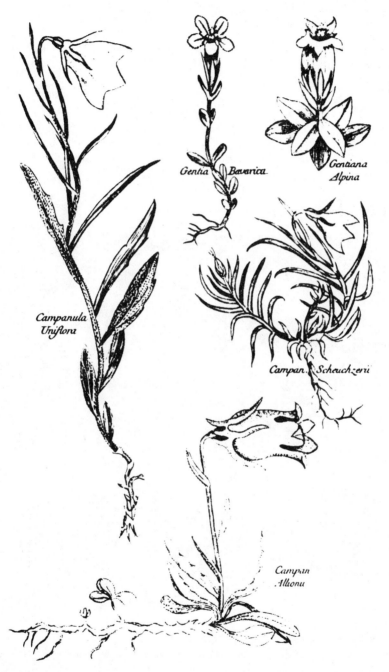

Gentia Bavarica

Gentiana Alpina

Campanula Uniflora

Campan. Scheuchzeru

Campan Allionu

Flore du Dauphiné — 18ème siècle. (2) Alpine flowers of the 18th century.

19

Modern transportation has greatly influenced the development of liqueurs. To ensure that certain products are absolutely fresh, they are brought in by trucks, train or plane within 24 hours of their harvest. To guard against possible shortages, plantations have been created in new areas where climactic variations are constant. This has made exotic fruits and spices readily available at competitive prices.

These precautions are taken to make certain that the ingredients used are invariably the same; the same species of seeds, of fruits and of spices. All this leads to one requirement: the quality of the plant, herb or fruits must be optimum at the moment when it is processed. This is what gives it its essential quality; its distinct identity.

La salle des plantes. The room where the Carthusian monks preserve and keep the 130 different kinds of herbs and plants needed to make their various liqueurs.

What Keeps It All Together, The "Water of Life"

The ethereal spirit trapped by the alchemists was thought to posess magical powers, to be the essence of life itself. It became quickly known as the "elixir of life" or the "brandy devil" depending on its results, whether it cured or doomed. In the Middle Ages the term "aqua vitae" was generally used to describe this liquid spirit. At about the same time there appeared in Ireland a Gaelic expression "uisge beatha," the derivation of the word "whiskey." At the end of the XVIIth century all spirits were still called "waters," and "waters of life." "Aqua vitae" survives today as "eau-de-vie" in France, "aquavit" in Sweden, Norway and Denmark. The Russians called it "vodka"; meaning little water, a term of affection for this special water that restores life. In Spanish, what remains is the concrete description of the burning sensation of the spirit; "hot water" became "fire water" or "aguardiente."

Whatever those spirits were called, they were all strong and fiery and they were all obtained through distillation.

The word distillation comes from the Latin "destillare," which means falling or flowing drop by drop: trickling down. This is in fact what happens in distillation. The process is one of turning a liquid into vapor by heating it, then bringing it back to liquid form by condensation, drop by drop.

Distillation separates by means of fire. In closed vessels the essentials oils of any substance separates from the other, heavier parts by taking advantage of differences in volatility. The object of distillation is to purify substances or to arrive at a new liquid which fuses the desired essential oils of all the substances involved.

Although the practice of distillation goes back very far, it doesn't seem to have been known in the pre-Christian world. The Alexandrian alchemists used distillation quite frequently, and Zosimus of Panopolis, a prolific writer of the 5th century speaks of the distillation of a "divine water" or "panacea." Mary, the Jewess, or Prophetess as she is sometimes referred to, had a well-known school of alchemists in Alexandria. They experimented with distillation, but how could Mary have guessed that she would not be remembered in the laboratory as a great scientist, but in the modern kitchen, as a double-boiler, the Bain-Marie.

The Arabs improved the earlier apparatus. Through distillation, they transformed wine into alcohol, extracted various ethereal oils from plants and plant juices, and purified water.

By the XIIIth century, distillation was common knowledge among the alchemists, the scholars and the apothecaries in Europe. But alcohol, a distilled spirit obtained from any organic compound formed by fermentation, was at that time usually made from wine. It was only in the XVth century that research widened the horizon and alcohol from grain and fruits was distilled. In the XVIth century brandy or "burned wine" was discovered. The common apparatus used was the alembic or simple Pot Still.

In a Pot Still alcohol is distilled in two separate vessels at a relatively low proof —130/140.* Much of the original flavor of the substance involved is retained because it is a slow and controllable process. It is easy to stop, either to remove unwanted elements or to add and put back those that are necessary. Today, distillation in a Pot Still is often required by law or tradition, as in the case of Cognacs, Armagnacs or Whiskeys.

A discovery in the early XIXth century played a major role in improving the purity of the product. In 1830, Mr. Coffey perfected a system of continuous distillation also called the Patent Still method. With this apparatus, alcohol is rectified: purified by renewed or continuous distillation. The result is a strong and relatively pure neutral spirit or alcohol with very little left of the basic flavor and character.

This spirit can be made from any ingredient such as grain, fruits or plants, but it is almost always distilled from grain. The variety of these spirits is great since they can be blended together. These neutral spirits are distilled at or above 190 proof, and are purified in the Still to a minimum 95% absolute alcohol purity. They have no odor, no flavor and no body. They are used in the blending of other spirits and as a base for liqueurs. The two most closely related are gin and vodka.

Gin is a neutral spirit combined with aromatic substances; the flavor of juniper berries gives it its main characteristics. Most gins are not aged.

Vodka, originally made from potatoes, is now made from grain. The neutral spirit is further purified by charcoal filtering which adds a subtle flavor. Vodkas are not aged, and most of them have no discernable taste.

Akvavit, a barley and potato distillate is clear, colorless and very potent. It is a Scandinavian drink originally made in Aalborg, Denmark.

Whiskeys are produced from the same substance as grain neutral spirits. They are usually distilled in a Pot Still from fermented mash of grain, a grain steeped in hot water to moisten the starch and start the fermentation. Then they mature in wood barrels for a minimum period of 4 years.

Remember that all distilled spirits are colorless and that it is the aging and the maturing in wood barrels that gives color, bouquet and smoothness to the liquor.

* To define the alcoholic content of spirits and liqueurs proof is used in the U.S., Gay-Lussac degrees in France and the Sykes proof system in the U.K. The equivalent of 100 Gay-Lussac degrees (100% alcohol) is 200 US proof or 175.25 British proof.

Scotch, made only in Scotland, is distilled mainly from barley. Its characteristic smokey flavor is due to the roasting of barley with peat as fuel. The blend is then placed in wood casks that had previously contained sherry wine. It is aged at least 4 years. The greatest scotches age for 12 years.

Irish is made only in Ireland and is distilled from barley as well. Barley is dried in kilns. The smoke never comes in contact with the grain.

Bourbon, **Rye** and **Corn Whiskies** are made in the U.S.

Bourbon is distilled from a mash composed of at least 51% corn. It matures in newly charred oak barrels.

Rye, is distilled from a mash containing at least 51% rye grain. It also matures in newly charred oak barrels.

Corn is distilled from a mash containing at least 80% corn, and it matures in uncharred or reused charred barrels.

Fruits are used to make what are called fruit distillates, fruit brandies or "eaux-de-vie." Fruits can be processed by using the Pot Still (alembic) which is the slower distillation, or the Patent Still method which produces higher proof distillates. The best known of all fruit distillates is made from grapes. Brandy is a term which derives from the expression "burned wine" because of the fire used in the distillation. It is generally thought of as the alcoholic spirit made from mash of grapes, but any other fruit can be used.

Brandy (made from grapes) is aged for different periods in white oak barrels which gives it its smooth characteristics, its bouquet and its golden color.

Cognac is a brandy produced and bottled exclusively in the Cognac region of France. Today, as in the past, it is distilled in Pot Stills and it goes through two non-continuous distillations.

Armagnac, as opposed to cognac, which is blended, is a straight brandy. It is distilled from grapes grown in the Gers region in Southern France. It is distilled once only and aged for several years.

Marc is a brandy distilled from the residue of the wine press after the grapes have been pressed.

Grappa is the Italian version of marc. It is distilled from the skins of the grapes once they have been crushed for the making of wine.

The other fruit brandies are usually known as "alcools blancs" because they are colorless and the result of rectification. A fruit brandy is usually identified by the name of its main ingredient: *Pear Williams* is a pear brandy, *Mirabelle* is the name of the small plum from which the brandy is made, *Framboise* a raspberry brandy, *Kirsch*, the German name for cherry, describes a cherry brandy, *Slivovitz* is the name of a plum brandy from Eastern Europe. At least two fruit brandies acquire a nice golden warm color as the result of aging:

Apple-jack distilled from the mash of apples is the best known and most typical fruit brandy in the U.S. Apples are crushed, distilled and aged.

Calvados: an apple-jack made in Normandy and aged about 4 years.

Spirits are also made from plants. The best known are the sugar cane and the heart of the mexcal cactus.

24

Rum   is distilled from a mash of sugar cane, sugar cane syrup, sugar cane molasses or any other sugar cane product.

There are basically two types of rums: The light, dry high-proof rum from Puerto Rico and Cuba used in many cocktails, and the heavier rums at a lower proof from the West Indies. Arrach is a type of rum from South East Asia distilled from sugar cane, rice or the sap of palm.

Tequila   is distilled from the fermented mash of the heart (pina) of the mezcal cactus, a giant pineapple like plant, cultivated around the small village of Tequila in Mexico.

The Golden Syrup, The Lacing

Dates, figs, honey and cane have always been treasured for their sweet and pleasant flavor. They were known to give energy as well as to produce a mild and delicious euphoria after being left in water. Of course they were also used as remedies.

The date palm was already flourishing in Sumer. One could even venture to date it as far back as 5000BC. The tree was useful and very easy to take care of. It grew along the numerous irrigation canals in fertile valleys such as those of the Tigris, the Euphrates and of the Nile. The fruit could be eaten fresh or dried. Juice, syrup or wine could be made from the fruit of the sap of the tree and be used to preserve other food as well.

Figs were popular but not as versatile as dates. They proliferated in the hotter climates and their mild laxative properties made them the favorites of the Egyptians. They seemed to help the ever—fasting Egyptians who thought most illnesses came from the intestines which should therefore be cleansed as often as possible.

Until the end of the Middle Ages and the early Renaissance, when sugar cane invaded Europe, so to speak, the qualities of honey made it the preferred sweetener. The "Route of Honey" went westward as the Aryans introduced it on their way to India, where it was enjoyed for its taste and color. India already had a sweetening agent, sugar cane. Honey, being pure sugar, ferments easily, into "mead", one of the oldest drinks and a favorite of England until the 16th century. Because the monastery doors were then closed, beeswax candles were no longer needed for worship, and the bees were driven out into the countryside.

It appears that cane, coming from the East, crossed roads with honey. The Chinese knew about sugar cane and used the "sap of certain reeds" to make their sweets. In India a cube of sugar would top a meal. It was also served with fruits and yogurt or cheese as dessert. When the Arabs conquered Spain and started to influence Europe, they brought with them, among other favorite foods, sugar cane, and began to cultivate it on the Mediterranean shores. They were successful where the climate was favorable, and from the island of Cyprus and Madeira, areas rich in fruits, came the first candied fruits and bonbons.

Until the 16th century and the expansion of the sugar cane production in the New World, sugar was a luxury sold in minute quantities, known only to the learned and the rich —the scribes, the scholars, and the kings. Sugar was transported and sold in loaves of 18 to 20 pounds. The whiter the loaf, the better the quality. Some areas in the Near

East used to cook it with milk to give it an extra shine and sell it at a higher price.

Throughout the Renaissance, Italian banquets were famous for the intricacy and magnificence of their spun sugar sculptures. It is not surprising that the Italians were free "to fantasize" in sugar: they had managed to monopolize the trade. It took the perfect climate of the West Indies and the vision of the conquistadors to spread the cultivation of sugar cane and to make it more easily available to all of Europe.

It was only in the beginning of the 19th century, during the English Blockade which ended all trade with the West Indies and South East Asia, that Europe had to search for a sugar cane substitute. Then, under Napoleon's urgings, sugar produced from a root plant was developed on a large enough scale that several countries soon became self-sufficient.

Sugar became even more important when people began to realize that fruit and food could be preserved with it; jams and jellies could be made with it; that flower and fruit pastes were exquisite. They discovered what others had known many centuries before, that liqueurs and aromatized wines tasted better with sugar.

The virtues of sugar had often been disregarded. Sailors cruising the oceans suffered greatly, not only from a lack of vitamin c but also from a lack of sugar. Their diets consisted mainly of salt and starches.

Golden, sweet syrup mixed with alcohol and spiced with herbs is part of a tradition still very much alive. In liqueurs and cordials a sweetener accomplishes several purposes; it moderates the acidity of certain fruits, it softens the bitterness of some plants while bringing their individual perfumes to the fore.

Today its use in liqueurs is regulated by law and is also regulated by each specific formula arrived at through years of experience.

Making Sweet and Powerful Drinks

The various ingredients of a particular formula determine which process is used in the making of a liqueur, but it always involves several stages. To facilitate the first step in making a liqueur, fruits, plants or whatever ingredients are used have to be prepared; fruits are pitted, crushed, stemmed or peeled, plants are cleaned, sorted out and inspected.

The first and most important stage is the extraction of the basic aroma and flavor of the main ingredient(s) with the help of a spirit. This can be achieved through maceration or infusion alone. Then comes the distillation. The two operations can either be separate or combined. The method chosen has to bring out the best of the aromatic substances, the essential oils. Therefore the choice will depend on the nature of the raw material. The extract from the ingredients is recognized as the liqueur's identity. The result is called aromatized spirits or infusions depending on the process used.

Maceration is a cold process used for ingredients that do not evaporate rapidly, that are so delicate, that even a low temperature may affect their stability. Such is the case of the most tender of fresh fruits such as peaches, raspberries, or bananas. The fruits might be burned by the heat of the distillation.

Maceration, a single process, consists of steeping the soft fruits (and all the ingredients of a given formula) in tanks of high proof spirits such as brandy, neutral spirits or others. Maceration ends when the spirit has absorbed all the bouquet and flavors of the mixture. It can take several weeks or several months for the perfume to be absorbed, and for the aromatic substances to infuse the spirit with all their flavor and magnificent bouquet.

Infusion is used mainly for dry leaves and plants. First they have to be moistened, and when they have softened, covered with a heated spirit. Infusion and maceration are not unlike the brewing of tea. They both involve aromatic substances placed directly in the spirit.

In some instances, a system that resembles the percolation of coffee is used. Spirits are put at the bottom of the tank. Then the heated spirit is pumped up and sprayed over the aromatic substances placed at the top. The spirit infused with some of the flavor drips back down and the process is repeated until all the flavor has been extracted.

Distillation is a hot process used when the flavoring ingredients, flowers, plants seeds or fruit rinds, have been dried. It is also best suited for herbs and roots rich in oils that can only be extracted when heated. Distillation, the process of separating less volatile substances from others, accentuates the flavor and produces a deeper aroma. It concentrates. And even though it is the process used for making spirits such as whiskeys, neutral spirits, rum or tequila it is but a stage in the making of a liqueur. The range of basic ingredients for a liqueur is usually a combination of fruits, herbs, spices and plants.

The distillate is very high proof and like all distillates, is colorless.

The distillation process is described very appropriately as a "run". It imparts the spirit with the flavor of the ingredients. The beginning and end of a run (head and tail) are unstable and carry all kinds of impurities. It is important to eliminate them since they are the cause of the "headaches" one might get when drinking less purified spirits.

When a second distillation takes place the so-called "heart" of the distillate is purified once more so that the resulting liqueur is indeed a very pure product.

Once the ingredients have yielded their flavor and aroma into various spirits or infusions (depending on the process used), the formula dictates in detail the final dosage, and records the proportions needed for each liqueur to acquire its unique character.

In some cases the mixture of these different aromatized spirits or infusions is blended further with another spirit, be it brandy, rum or another.

Then the final touch is added: the golden syrup.

At this point the extraction of the perfumes and the blending of the basic elements is achieved.

The liqueur is then filtered to achieve brilliance and shine, and cut at the desired proof with distilled water. Sometimes, when the formula demands it, a liqueur is placed in old vats for a certain period of time to achieve the complete fusion of the ingredients and acquire a rich bouquet and a suggestive color. The spirit acquired in the vats not only the flavor and aroma of the fruit, but its marvellous color as well. If the ingredients were macerated, the liqueur is now ready for its long journey into the world, and does not need aging. Distilled products are colorless. Natural vegetable coloring, such as saffron if yellow or gold is desired, or plant extracts for emerald green, is added. Color satisfies an esthetic sense, pleasing the imagination when the name of a fruit or herb brings out a very concrete image of the fruit or field.

High Standards of Quality

European liqueurs have achieved wordly fame. The standards of quality and consistency set by the first modern liqueur makers are still aspired to by today's distillers.

In France, until World War II, liqueurs were graded, not as the wines with "Appellations controlées" but according to other standards. They were classified according to sweetness and alcoholic strength. Some such as *Creams, Oils* or *Balms* had a thick and oily consistency, others such as *Waters, Extracts* and *Elixirs* were much lighter. Liqueurs were also classified according to quality as *Ordinaire, Semi-Fine, Fine* or *Superfine*.

Today such a classification does not exist. Liqueurs and cordials are one, but a distinction is made between **Creams, Liqueurs** and **Fruit Flavored Brandies.**

Creams are sweeter, heavier and denser. It is a common appellation for some liqueurs with a smooth and creamy consistency. Originally and literally "cream" means of the top, of the best, "la crème de la crème", and as such, the category of creams transcends all others. Once can find a cream of violet, of cocoa, of cassis, of banana or of almond, to name only a few.

Fruit Liqueurs are made with neutral grain or cane spirit. These leave the flavor and the aroma of the fruit intact. They can be bottled at any desired proof.

Fruit Flavored Brandies are liqueurs. It is a special classification unique to the U.S. These liqueurs are made with a brandy base as opposed to grain or cane spirits, and have to be at least 70 proof.

There is a marked difference between a fruit liqueur and a fruit flavored brandy of the same fruit. They are blended with different spirits and they differ in proof. While the proof of a fruit flavored brandy is regulated by law, a liqueur is at a proof which brings out the best qualities of the fruit. So, for a particular fruit such as cherry, you will have a choice of a cherry brandy (called usually Kirsch or Kirschwasser), a cherry liqueur (such as Peter Heering), or a cherry flavored brandy.

30

Secret Formulas, Remnants Of A Not So Distant Past

Every manufacturer of liqueur in the world aspires to produce a complete line of liqueurs, varying from 15 to 35 flavors (sounds like ice-cream?). Most of the liqueurs are generic types and even though the basic ingredient is the same and the principle the same, each has its own secret formula.

In each liqueur there is in general not one basic ingredient but a variety of ingredients. They are usually not made with one type of fruit or seed, or one predominant flavor, but depending on the formula, with many types of seeds, spices, fruits or a combinaton of them. The quality of the ingredients, a slight change in the formula, all these factors explain the basic difference in taste between several *crèmes de cacao* or *cranberry liqueurs* or *blackberry flavored brandies*.

The formulae are intricate, most of them are secret, some have been transmitted from generation to generation. They are basically the same as they were centuries ago. A few adjustments had to be made to satisfy a drier taste in drinks. They require a high degree of expertise and know how, they are guarded as jealously as the doors to Paradise. "Perfect formulas" were discovered after long years of research and no one will let the fruit of such arduous labor fall easily into "foreign" hands. It reminds one of the secrecy that surrounded the work of earlier alchemists and the initiation necessary to be admitted into that privileged circle of knowledge.

Now that we have taken you on a trip through history and many continents, maybe you'll feel inclined to follow the example of Des Esseintes, the hero of a well known French novel, "A Rebours" by J.K. Huysmans:

> He made his way to the dining-room, where there was a
> cupboard built into one of the walls containing a row of little

31

barrels, resting side-by-side on tiny sandalwood stands and each broached at the bottom with a silver spigot.

This collection of liqueur casks he called his mouth organ.

A rod could be connected to all the spigots, enabling them to be turned by one and the same movement, so that once the apparatus was in position it was only necessary to press a button concealed in the wainscoting to open all the conduits simultaneously and so fill with liqueur the minute cups underneath the taps.

The organ was then open. The stops labelled 'flute', 'horn', and 'vox angelica' were pulled out, ready for use. Des Esseintes would drink a drop here, another there, playing internal symphonies to himself, and providing his palate with sensations analogous to those which music dispenses to the ear.

PART III

A VOYAGE THROUGH THE WORLD OF LIQUEURS

Before take off...
A few words of advice

You will need some standard equipment:

mixing glass and hand strainer,
shaker with built-in strainer,
long stirring spoon,
ice bucket,
sharp knife,
cork screw,
lime and lemon squeezer,
metal jiggers,
measuring spoon,
short straws.

2107721

It's nice to have a *blender,* but elbow grease can replace it.
A *chafing dish* for flambé dishes and fondues is also handy.

Glasses

Our medieval ancestors drank out of gold, silver and pewter goblets. Later, in affluent households, there was a glass for every kind of beverage. It was a must to have silverware, china and glassware adapted to every occasion. Today everyday life is somewhat simplified. What's important is how the glass fits in your hand, how it enhances the color, fragrance and taste of the liqueur.

Snifters of an average size (4 to 6 oz.), neither too small nor too large, seem to fullfil these conditions whether you drink the liqueur straight or on the rocks.

Use champagne glasses or cocktail glasses for frappés, cocktails served on shaved or crushed ice, or for strained drinks.

Use old fashioned glasses for cocktails on the rocks and tall glasses for long drinks.

Wine glasses, cordial and liqueur glasses are also useful.

These are suggestions and not rules. If you have a favorite glass, by all means use it.

When expecting company put the glasses in the freezer. Frosting adds a special quality to a glass or to a cocktail. For sweet drinks, try coating the rim of the glass with lemon juice and sugar before storing it in the freezer. When using a lemon, or orange twist, rub it along the rim of the glass, then twist it over the drink.

A few explanations:

Frappé means a liqueur served in a champagne or cocktail glass full of crushed ice and sipped through a short straw.

Flambé means setting a liqueur aflame. Use a long match and warm the liqueur before flaming. If you use a low proof liqueur, add a tablespoon of brandy, bourbon, scotch or vodka.

Pousse-café is a rainbow cordial, an after dinner drink made of differently colored liqueurs poured slowly and carefully, one at a time, in a tall narrow cordial glass. The trick is for the ingredients *not to combine* but to float on top of each other. You can use as few as two liqueurs and as many as seven, but start with the heaviest. It is extremely difficult to determine the weight of various liqueurs since densities for the same flavor vary from one manufacturer to another. Like the alchemists and early distillers, you will have to proceed by trial and error, and you will succeed.

Here are two possible combinations:

1/4 ounce green crème de menthe at the bottom
1/4 ounce yellow Chartreuse
1/4 ounce Peter Heering
1/4 ounce brandy or cognac
or
1/4 ounce crème d'amande
1/4 ounce green crème de menthe
1/4 ounce Cointreau

The variations are infinite. Good luck!

RECIPES FOR DRINKS ARE FOR ONE, UNLESS OTHERWISE SPECIFIED

A Taste of Wild Herbs

CHARTREUSE

The word Chartreuse comes from the religious order of the Chartreux. It was a cloistered and contemplative order living in solitude, silence and prayer. However, from the time the order was founded, the monks knew how to combine scholarly and spiritual pursuits and the reality of living off their environment. They had their souls turned toward God but their feet solidly planted on the ground. They lived like hermits but, at times, they opened their doors to the outside world. This is how, through rather unusual circumstances, they became the makers of Chartreuse.

The mystery of Chartreuse starts with the name of its inventor. He probably was a XVIth century French alchemist, who was well aware of the virtues of plants. He chose 130 different ones. In 1605, the Maréchal D'Estrées gave the manuscript containing the recipe for this special elixir to the Chartreux of Vauvert, a monastery near Paris. The Maréchal D'Estrées did this in memory of his beautiful wife, Gabrielle. A magnificent painting of Gabrielle D'Estrées in her bath, hangs on the walls of the château of Azay-Le-Rideau on the Loire River; she was the mistress of King Henry IV, and it is easy to understand when looking at the painting why he fell violently in love with her. The young woman, who died at an early age under mysterious circumstances, was said to have been fond of liqueurs. It would have been so easy and in line with the times to have doctored her drinks—enemies are so crafty!

In 1737 the document containing the elixir of the Maréchal D'Estrées reached La Grande Chartreuse, the mother house of the order. Frère Jérôme Maubec, the convent apothecary, was put in charge of finding a practical way to manufacture this elixir for purely medicinal purposes. Since the monks were providing medical care for their tenants the herb-based liqueurs were developed to cure the sick.

Alcohol was then considered more a medicine or a disinfectant, than an enjoyable drink. Frère Jérôme was about to succeed, when he fell seriously ill and hardly had time to give the essential details of his research to a friar, before he died. Frère Antoine continued the work. In 1767, he finally wrote down the definite formula of a Health Elixir (l'elixir de santé, the ancestor of the present green Chartreuse). It enjoyed an immediate popularity. The adventures of the Chartreuse went on for a long time. During the French Revolution, monks were persecuted and imprisoned, and the recipe passed from one monk to another until it ended up in the possession of Dom Basile. The order was dispersed. Dom Basile did not know what to do with the precious document, so he sold it for very little money to an apothecary in Grenoble. By then, Napoleon had decided that all secret remedies should be given to the Ministry of the Interior. The apothecary sent the formula to Paris. The bureaucracy did not take it seriously and sent it back to him. The elixir began to be manufactured discreetly in Grenoble. In 1817, the monks were allowed to go back to their monastery. They retrieved the original manuscript, and distillation started again in the Convent. In 1838, Frère Bruno Jaquet discovered a new sister liqueur: the yellow Chartreuse. Many people have tried to steal the formula since, but nobody has yet succeeded.

DRINKS

Chartreuse on the rocks
Chartreuse and club soda
Orange Chartreuse
Blueberry Chartreuse

You can also use grapefruit, melon, raspberry, or lemon juice in the following proportions:
1/3 Green Chartreuse
2/3 Fruit Juice

You can add club soda to fruit juice and Chartreuse if you feel so inclined.

Chartreuse and tonic

Chartreuse and scotch:
2 oz. Yellow Chartreuse
2 oz. Scotch

Chartreuse and vodka:
2 oz. vodka
2 oz. Green Chartreuse
Pour vodka in a glass and pour Chartreuse on top without mixing. It will float on top.

Well chilled very dry Champagne with a dash of Yellow or Green Chartreuse.

Swampwater, invented in the United States and most delectable.
1/3 Green Chartreuse
2/3 pineapple juice
Juice of a quarter of a lime
Mix well and serve over ice.

Le Verre Vert. Green Chartreuse on the rocks.

ENTREES

NOTE: Now that you are ready to discover or rediscover the pleasures of Chartreuse, we would like to make a suggestion: never use too much Chartreuse. It is a potent liqueur; you want it to complement rather than dominate the other ingredients. So do not exceed the proportions given in the following recipes. Use the same proportions for your own recipes.
Do not add Chartreuse while the dish is on the fire.

SAUTEED SHRIMP WITH CHARTREUSE

2 lbs. medium shrimp
4 tbsps. butter
2 tbsps. orange juice, strained
salt, white pepper
3 tbsps. Green Chartreuse
Ring of rice and peas
1 cup heavy cream (optional)

Shell and devein the shrimp, rinse them, and dry them well with paper towelling. Heat the butter in a large skillet. Add the shrimp and cook them briskly for 5 minutes, turning them frequently until they are uniformly pink and cooked through. Sprinkle them with the orange juice and season them with salt and pepper to taste. Reduce the heat to low.

In a small saucepan gently heat the Chartreuse, set it ablaze, and pour it flaming over the shrimp. Shake the pan until the flame expires. Unmold the ring of rice and peas onto a warm serving platter and fill the center with the shrimp. Serve at once. A sauce to be served with the shrimp may be quickly prepared by blending into the cooking juices remaining in the skillet 1 cup of heavy cream, and an additional tablespoon of Chartreuse. Season to taste with salt and pepper. Serves 6.

CHICKEN SUPREME CHARTREUSE

1/4 lb. sweet butter
1 cup bacon - diced
8 shallots - finely chopped
4 chicken breasts - halved,
 skinned, deboned and cut into
 strips
2 cups mushrooms - sliced
1/2 cup dry white wine
1/2 cup chicken stock
2 tbsps. Green Chartreuse
1 tbsp tarragon
4 oz. heavy cream
salt and pepper
parsley - finely chopped

Melt butter in large heavy frying pan over medium high heat. Add bacon and shallots and saute for 3 minutes. Add chicken strips and continue to saute until slightly browned. Add mushrooms, stock, and wine. When liquid starts to simmer, reduce heat to low, add Chartreuse and cover. Simmer for about 10 minutes until chicken is cooked through. Season with salt and pepper and finish with tarragon and heavy cream mixing thoroughly.

Serve on a bed of fluffy white rice and garnish with parsley. Serves 4.

BAKED FRESH HAM IN CHARTREUSE

4 to 6 lbs fresh ham (leg of pork)
1/2 teaspoon dried chervil
12 to 18 small potatoes, peeled
4 tbsps. Green Chartreuse

Preheat oven to 350⁰. Remove the skin of the fresh ham. If you like, roast it separately until crisp, for cocktail snacks. Trim the ham of excess fat, leaving a layer about 1/4 inch thick. Score the top in a diamond pattern, rub it with the chervil, and sprinkle it with salt and pepper to taste.

Cook the ham, uncovered, in a baking pan in the oven, 30 minutes per lb for a whole ham, 40 minutes per lb for a half ham, or until a meat thermometer inserted in the thickest part of the meat registers 185⁰. Add the potatoes during the last 45 minutes of cooking. When they are tender and browned, remove them to a saucepan on top of the stove along with some of the drippings from the roasting pan. Keep the potatoes warm over low heat. Sprinkle the ham with 2 tbsps Chartreuse and continue cooking for 5 minutes. Sprinkle with the remaining liqueur and cook for a final 5 minutes. Remove the ham from the oven, and place in a warm serving platter. Let it rest for 10 minutes before carving. Drain the potatoes and serve them with the ham, along with braised lettuce. Serves 10.

DESSERTS

NEIGE A LA CHARTREUSE

4 eggs: separate carefully the
  whites from the yolks
4 level tbsps. sugar
1 wine glass Green Chartreuse

Cook egg yolks with sugar until it is lemon yellow and coats the spoon. Add a wine glass of Green Chartreuse. Mix well. Cool. Beat the egg whites until they peak. Stir half of the white in the yolks mixture and fold in the other half.

Pour into a mold or platter. Cook at 400⁰ for 15 to 20 minutes until the color is a golden brown. Serve at once. (You can use a regular souffle dish but then let it cook a little longer since a souffle dish is deeper than a platter). Serves 4.

CHARTREUSE BAVARIAN CREAM WITH STRAWBERRIES

1 packet gelatine
1/4 cup water, cold
1/4 cup sugar
1/2 tbsp salt
2½ cups milk
2 eggs
1 cup whipping cream
1/4 cup Green Chartreuse
fresh strawberries

Soften 1 packet (1 tbsp) unflavored gelatin in 1/4 cup cold water. Combine the softened gelatine with 1/4 cup sugar and 1/2 tbsp salt in a saucepan. Add 2-1/2 cups of milk, and 2 egg yolks slightly beaten. Beat well.

Cook over medium heat stirring constantly, for about 6 to 7 minutes, until mixture coats a metal spoon. Chill until slightly thickened. Whip 1 cup whipping cream and fold it, along with 1/4 cup Chartreuse, into the gelatine mixture. Pour the cream into a chilled 5 cup mold and chill until firm, 3 to 4 hours.

To serve, unmold the cream on a large chilled serving dish. Top each serving with sliced or whole fresh strawberries. Serves 6 to 8.

CITRON CHARTREUSE SOUFFLE

2 envelopes unflavored gelatin
1/2 cup cold water
6 eggs
2/3 cup sugar
  Pinch salt
1 tablespoon grated lemon peel
2/3 cup lemon juice
3 tablespoons Green Chartreuse
2 cups heavy cream
1/4 cup coarsely chopped
  pistachio nuts
Lemon pinwheel

Prepare 1½ quart souffle dish with 4-inch foil collar.

In small saucepan, sprinkle gelatin over water; let stand 10 minutes to soften. Place saucepan over low heat until gelatin dissolves. Remove from heat; cool.

In a large mixing bowl, beat eggs, sugar and salt until thick and light (about 8 minutes).

To cooled gelatin mixture add lemon peel, lemon juice and Green Chartreuse. Pour into egg mixture; fold until well-blended. Refrigerate 5-10 minutes until mixture begins to mound.

Beat 1½ cups cream until stiff peaks form. Fold into lemon mixture until no white streaks are left. Pour mixture into prepared souffle dish. Refrigerate at least 3 hours.

When ready to serve, carefully remove foil collar. Beat remaining cream. Decorate top of souffle with additional whipped cream and lemon pinwheel. Lightly press chopped pistachio nuts around sides.
Serves 8.

Citron Souffle Chartreuse

45

AFTER DINNER DRINKS

Straight or on the rocks

A Cardinal:
2/3 Green Chartreuse
1/3 Yellow Chartreuse

An Episcopal:
1/3 Green Chartreuse
2/3 Yellow Chartreuse

THE ABBEY AT FÉCAMP, FRANCE
The Home of Bénédictine

BENEDICTINE

Sitting with the bottle in front of him[Des Esseintes]had spent hours thinking about the monks who sold it, the Benedictines of the Abbey of Fécamp . . . They forced themselves upon his imagination, looking just as if they had come straight out of the Middle Ages, growing medicinal herbs, heating retorts, distilling in alembics sovereign cordials, infallible panaceas.
"A Rebours" by J. K. Huysmans

At the beginning of the XVIth century, Dom Bernardo Vincelli lived in a Benedictine monastery in Fécamp, Normandy. Wild plants and herbs grew in profusion on the seaside cliffs: angelica, hyssop, wild mint, to cite only a few. Most of them are surrounded by legends. Angelica, for instance, means the plant of the angels. The story goes that an angel appeared to a monk in a vision and urged him to use angelica as a remedy against the ever-present plague and pestilence. Angelica was also used through the centuries for stomach pains or for clearing the eyes and ears. Today, the candied stems still decorate cakes and the leaves make tea. We don't know if Dom Bernardo also had a vision but he was determined to put to use the plants growing all around the monastery. He spent many hours trying to find the exact mixture of herbs from the sea cliffs and spices from the East to create a Benedictine elixir that would cure many ills. He was so exultant with the final result of his experiments that he had the following inscription put on the bottle DOM "DEO OPTIMO MAXIMO." (To God most good, most great.) It still stands nowadays on every botle of Bénédictine. And nobody has yet had any reason to take it off! Each bottle wears it well. King Francis I, a lover of good food and drink, tasted the new elixir and gave it his seal of approval. Dom Bernardo dispensed it as a tonic or restorative and as a digestive for tired and ailing monks, and also to the local farmers against malaria and assorted diseases. During the French Revolution, religious orders were scattered in all directions, the monasteries ruined, the casks emptied and the formula was lost. A distinguished merchant from Fécamp, Alexandre Legrand, rediscovered the lost recipe among long-hidden ancient manuscripts in 1863.

It contained the flavor of 27 herbs and dried plants, ceylon tea, juniper berries, myrrh, angelica, cinnamon, cloves, nutmeg and vanilla on a neutral spirits base. The production of Bénédictine has remained in the hands of the Legrand family ever since. Alexandre Legrand was so pleased with his discovery that he built a fairy tale Renaissance type palace in Fécamp to house the distillery, aging caves, and a very interesting museum. Bénédictine has fallen into secular hands but its secret is as well kept as when it remained inside the walls of a monastery.

DRINKS

Bénédictine on the rocks.
Bénédictine with soda water.

The Sundowner:
1 oz. Bénédictine
1 oz. vodka
4½ oz. orange juice
1/2 oz. lemon juice
Pour over ice cubes in a tall glass. Stir lightly and sip.

The Moonglow:
1 oz. Bénédictine
1 oz. vodka
2 oz. grapefruit juice
Pour over ice cubes in an old fashioned glass. Stir well.

The Queen Elizabeth:
1 oz. Bénédictine
2 ozs. sweet vermouth
the juice of half a lime
Shake well with ice, strain into cocktail glass.

ENTREES

BARBECUED CHICKEN BENEDICTINE

2/3 cup peanut oil
1/3 cup Bénédictine
1/4 teaspoon thyme leaves
1/4 teaspoon rosemary
1/8 teaspoon coarsely ground
  pepper
3 large chicken breasts, split
salt

In a small jar with tight fitting lid, combine peanut oil, Bénédictine, thyme, rosemary, and pepper. Cover and shake vigorously until thoroughly blended. Pour over chicken. Marinate 12 hours or overnight, turning occasionally.

Place chicken on grill over medium coals. Sprinkle with salt. Grill 45 minutes or until done, turning and basting occasionally with marinade.

This dish can also be cooked in an oven. Place the pan about 3 inches from the source of heat, turn often and baste with the marinade.

Barbecuing meat is an old American tradition dating back to the 18th century. Even turtles were barbecued in New York in the 18th and 19th centuries. There are two stories about the origins of the word: from the French de "barbe à queue," the practice of roasting whole animals from whiskers to tail on huge spits, or from the Spanish word "barbacoa" the name of the wooden spit on which the meat was roasted.

KABOBS BENEDICTINE

3 lbs. beef, pork or lamb cut into
 1½-2" cubes
Quartered tomatoes
Quartered onions
Whole mushrooms
Chunks of green pepper

Marinade
1 jigger Bénédictine
1½ tbs. lemon juice
1/2 cup olive oil
1/4 cup dry sherry
1 tsp. minced green onion
1 tsp. dried tarragon
1/4 tsp. freshly ground black
 pepper
1/4 tsp. dry mustard
1/4 tsp. salt
Cayenne pepper to taste

Simmer all marinade ingredients over low heat for 5 minutes, cool. Pour over cubed meat. Let stand 5 to 6 hours or overnight, stirring occasionally.

On six to eight 8-inch skewers, alternate meat cubes, quartered tomatoes and onions, whole mushrooms and chunks of green pepper. Barbecue to taste, basting frequently with remaining marinade. As a final gourmet touch when cooking is done, attach a cube of sugar which has been well-soaked in Bénédictine to the end of each skewer, light and serve. Serves 6 to 8.

The red copper alembics of the distillation room in the Carthusian Monastery.

DESSERTS

GLACE DE LUXE

3/4 cup sugar
4 egg yolks
2 cups milk
2 cups cream (whipped)
1/2 cup Bénédictine

Combine sugar, egg yolks. Add milk, cook slowly in double boiler, stirring constantly until mixture coats spoon.

Cool, add Bénédictine and fold in the whipped cream. Pour into refrigerator tray, freeze until firm. Serves 8.

MOCHA SPONGE CAKE

1 tbsp. (1 envelope) unflavored
  gelatin
1/4 cup cold water
1 tbsp. instant coffee
3/4 cup sugar
1¼ cups boiling water
2 tbsp. Benedictine (or B&B)
1 tbs. lemon juice
1/2 cup chopped toasted
  blanched almonds
1/2 cup toasted flaked coconut
2 egg whites, stiffly beatern
1 cup heavy cream

Soak gelatin in cold water 5 minutes to soften. Mix in sugar and instant coffee. Add boiling water; stir until mixture is dissolved. Stir in 1 table-spoon Bénédictine or (B&B) and lemon juice. Chill until thickened.

Set bowl of gelatin firmly in bowl of ice. Beat until very light and creamy. Fold in almonds and coconut, then fold in egg whites. Pour into a 6-cup mold. Chill until firm.
Unmold. Serve garnished with rosettes of heavy cream whipped with remaining 1 tablespoon liqueur
Serves 12.

AFTER DINNER DRINKS

Bénédictine straight or on the rocks.
Bénédictine with cognac.

Café Bénédictine:
*Put a dash of Bénédictine in your coffee
or drink it straight with your coffee.*

B & B
(Bénédictine and Brandy)

A long time ago, Bénédictine lovers discovered that brandy mixed with the liqueur gave a dry tang to Dom Bernardo's elixir. As the popularity of B&B grew, the Société Bénédictine in Fécamp made its own blend of Bénédictine and the finest Cognac.

DRINKS

B & B on the rocks.
B & B Stinger:
3 oz. B & B
1 oz. white crème de menthe.
Shake well with cracked ice, strain into a cocktail glass.

ENTREE

B & B MUSHROOM SOUP

1/2 pound fresh mushrooms
3 cups chicken broth
1 tablespoon cornstarch
2 tablespoons cold water
1/2 cup heavy cream
3 egg yolks, at room temperature
1/2 cup B&B Liqueur
Chopped chives

In covered blender container at medium speed, blend until smooth one third mushrooms and 1 cup broth; pour into large saucepan. Repeat with remaining mushrooms and broth. Cook over medium heat, stirring frequently, until mixture comes to a boil. Simmer 3 minutes.

Beat cream and egg yolks together with rotary beater until well blended. Stir cream mixture into the cooled soup. Stir in B&B Liqueur. Return to heat. Cook over medium-low heat,

stirring constantly, until mixture is
slightly thickened. To serve, garnish
with chopped chives.
It also may be chilled to serve cold.
Serves 5.

AFTER DINNER DRINKS

B & B with a demi-tasse.

B & B straight or on the rocks

B & B TEA: An exciting blend of the East and the West.
It is a light, natural drink, perfect after dinner or après-ski.

*For each serving, pour 6 oz. of freshly brewed
tea into a warmed 8 oz. stemglass. Add 1½ oz.
of B & B. Top with lightly whipped cream or whipped
topping. Sip through cream or topping.*

IZZARRA

Izarra means "star" in Basque. May it bring light, dreams and sparkles to your home, your kitchen, your friends and most importantly to yourself.

Izarra's particular flavour comes from flowers and herbs gathered in the Basque Pyrénées by the local population. Many of these plants don't grow any place else in the world, and the exact formula for Izarra is as unknown to us and to the world as the exact origins of the Basque language.

Izarra is the result of a long tradition. The Basque country was on the way to St. Jacques de Compostelle, the famous medieval shrine. For the pilgrims, the passage of the Pyrénées was one of the most arduous parts of the long journey. They used to buy elixirs from the local peasants to strengthen themselves or to soothe their tired bodies. When Louis XIII of France married Anne of Austria, the daughter of Philip III of Spain, there were numerous visits between the two countries, and one of these local elixirs called the liqueur des Pyrénées made its appearance at the French court where it was greatly appreciated. The old formula became commercialized in 1835. According to local folklore it has not changed. It was delicious then and it still is now!

DRINKS

Izarra on the rocks.
Izarra with tonic water and zest of lime or lemon.

The Pilgrim:
2 oz. Green Izarra (or Yellow)
1 oz. vodka

Pour over ice cubes, stir lightly

The Highland Shepherd:
1 oz. Izarra (Yellow)
1 oz. scotch

High Altitude:
1 oz. Izarra
2 oz. Italian vermouth
with or without tonic water

ENTREE

PORK PYRENEES

1 pkge (8 oz.) dried apricots
1 cup IZARRA Yellow
5 lbs. loin of pork roast
1 cup white wine
(or water)

Soak dried apricots in IZARRA for one hour. Sprinkle loin of pork with salt and pepper. Place in roasting pan, fat side up and roast in moderate oven for one hour. Remove fat from pan.

Arrange soaked apricots around roast. Pour over meat IZARRA Yellow and one cup of white wine or water so that apricots are covered. Roast for one hour longer basting several times. Place meat on platter and surround with apricots. Serve remaining pan juices separately. Serves 6.

DESSERTS

POACHED ORANGES

6 navel oranges
3/4 cup water
1 ½ cup sugar
1/4 cup Izarra Yellow

Peel rind and white membranes from oranges. Slice enough of orange rind to make about 4 tablespoons of slivers and combine with sugar and water. Cook syrup over a low flame, without stirring, for about eight minutes. Place oranges in hot syrup, basting constantly for about 5 minutes. Remove them from heat and add Izarra yellow. While oranges are chilling, baste with syrup. Serve very cold. Serves 6.

CHIFFON PIE IZARRA

6 eggs
2 cups heavy cream
1 tbsp. gelatin
1 cup sugar
1/2 cup cold water
1 crum or pastry shell
1/2 cup chopped pistachio nuts

Beat eggs and sugar. Add gelatin that has been dissolved in cold water and then melted over hot water. Whip cream until stiff. Fold into egg and gelatin mixture and add IZARRA Green. Pour into previously baked crumb or pastry shell. Sprinkle with chopped pistachio nuts and refrigerate for at least 2 hours. Serves 8.

AFTER DINNER DRINKS

Green and Yellow Izarra mixed together and served on ice, or straight.

MORE HERB LIQUEURS

Herb and spirits make a pleasing combination. It is not surprising that there are so many unusual herb liqueurs available:

Angel Elixir: galingale (mild ginger), cloves, nutmeg, orange peel, lemon peel, ginger, orris root, zedoary, cubebs and cardamom. These exotic aromatic ingredients are macerated in alcohol for several days. Then the liquid is filtered and distilled twice. Distilled rose water and sugar are then added.

Angelica cordial: cassia, cloves, lemon peels, lavender flowers, mace, marjoram, orange flowers, orange peel, orris root, juniper berries, rosemary leaves and vanilla are macerated in alcohol. After a few days, the liquid is filtered and sugar syrup added.

Calisay: over 120 different herbs, plants and fruits go into the making of this Spanish liqueur. Its secret has been in the hands of the same family for more than 250 years.

Cordial Médoc: a highly aromatic liqueur made in Bordeaux. Although it has a brandy base, it is flavoured with "Vin Vieux" (aged wine) which gives it a lovely maroon color.

Cuaranta y Tres (43): another Spanish liqueur which boasts 43 ingredients, but two liqueurs from Italy,

Centerbe and **Millefiori,** boast 100 and 1000 herbs, respectively.

Fior di Alpe: (flower of the Alps) a spicy gold Italian liqueur with a twig covered with silvery crystallized sugar inside the transparent narrow bottle.

Galliano: which has recently become very popular in the U.S. It's an Italian liqueur and a secret recipe of course: herbs, flowers, spices on a brandy base.

Make a barbecue sauce while you drink a "Harvey Wallbanger," a Galliano creation:

> 2 oz. vodka
> 4 oz. orange juice
> 1 oz. Galliano

Mix the vodka and the orange juice in a tall chilled glass, add ice cubes. Float Galliano on top.

Barbecue sauce:

2 cups ketchup
1 cup chili sauce
1/2 cup Worcestershire
1/2 cup Liquore Galliano
1/2 cup of dark brown sugar
1/4 cup lemon juice

Heat all ingredients together in saucepan. Keep hot as needed.

Jägermeister: a liqueur very popular in Germany: 56 herbs, root and fruit on a neutral spirit base. To really enjoy its dryness it should be served chilled. It goes very well with a glass of cool beer or with a touch of tonic water, ginger ale, bitter lemon or Coke.

Strega   means "witch" in Italian. Maybe its numerous ingredients will bewitch you. Try it with vodka.

Vieille-Cure   is a pale yellow and green liqueur, on a cognac and armagnac base. This potent drink comes from the Abbaye de Cenon in France.

Verveine du Velay   is similar to Chartreuse but with a more bitter vervain flavor. Verbena is supposed to have excellent digestive qualities. It was used as an ingredient in witches cauldrons to ward off evil spirits, and in love potions.

This by no means pretends to be an exhaustive description even if we add Aiguebelle, Trappistine, Claristine, Carmeline, Grignan, Elixir d'Anvers, de Spa, de Mondorf, de Montbazillac.

IRISH MIST

It is believed that at least four great Irish whiskies go into the preparation of Irish Mist. They are left to age in special warehouses and then honey, heather-honey, honies of foxgloves and clover are added. The final step is the careful addition of at least a dozen herbs. Irish Mist is made in Ireland and in Ireland only. It comes to us from Tulach Mohr.

In 1858, a young man by the name of Daniel Williams came to Dal's distillery in Tulach Mohr. In 1885, he took it over and created his own organization.

Williams wanted more than anything in the world to rediscover the formula for the ancient heather-wine, the legendary mead made of honey and spices, which had for centuries been the favorite drink of Irish poets and warriors. Its secret recipe had disappeared in 1691, in what is called in Irish history, "The Flight of the Wild Geese." After the Williamite wars, the elite of the Irish armies left their country to search for military service abroad. They went to Versailles, to the courts of Frédéric of Prussia and Maria Theresa of Austria. A few Irish officers rose to glory in the foreign armies.

For years with his son and grandson, William made countless experiments but could not recreate this historic drink. Then, in 1948, a traveler from Europe arrived at Tulach Mohr and he declared that he was in possession of the formula for heather-wine. But he never disclosed how he had come by it. It is said that he might have gotten it from the descendants of an Irish immigrant in Austria. The family experimented again, added some secret ingredients of their own, and Irish Mist was born.

DRINKS

On the rocks with a twist of lemon

Irish Mist and club soda:

1½ oz. Irish Mist
4 oz. club soda

O.J. Mist

1 oz. Irist mist
3 oz. orange juice
on the rocks.

Cup of Gold

1 oz. Irish Mist
3 oz. apple cider
Serve on the rocks. Garnish with apple slice.

Irish Mist Stinger

1 oz. Irish Mist
1 oz. white crème de menthe
Serve on cracked ice.

Irish Mist Sour

1 oz. Irish Mist
2 oz. chilled sour mix

Among other things, the Irish are famous for their toasts. Here are two of our favorites:

"Here is health to Ireland and all its counties and may everybody else be dead before the Irish"

"The health of the Salmon
A strong heart
And a wet mouth"

ENTREES

BEEF-BARLEY SOUP

2 lbs. beef soup bones
8 cups water
1 tbsp. salt
1 tsp. pepper
2 medium carrots, grated
1/4 cup barley
2 medium stalks celery,
  thinly sliced
1 medium onion, chopped
1/2 cup Irish Mist
1 can (16 oz.) whole tomatoes,
  chopped

In large saucepan place soup bones, water, salt and pepper. Bring to boil, reduce heat, simmer 2 hours or until meat is tender.

Remove meat from bones, trim fat. Cut into small chunks.

Return to broth in pan. Add remaining ingredients. Simmer 1 hour. Serves 6.

HANNIBULL BURGERS

2 lbs. ground chuck
1/2 tsp. salt
1/4 tsp. pepper
1/4 cup heavy cream
2 tbsps. minced fresh shallots
1/4 lb. fresh mushrooms, sliced
1/4 cup Irish Mist
1/2 cup heavy cream
1 large tomato, diced
2 tbsps. minced parsley
1/4 tsp. basil
1 tsp. salt

Mix ground chuck, salt, pepper, and cream together lightly. Shape into six patties.

In large skillet, pan-broil patties until cooked as desired. Remove to heated platter.

Cook shallots in pan drippings until soft. Add remaining ingredients. Stir until just heated through.

Serve beef patties on bed of rice. Pour sauce over all. Serves 6.

BAKED ACORN SQUASH

2 medium acorn squash,
  cut in half
1 lb. pork sausage meat
2 tbsps. dry bread crumbs
1/2 cup diced apple
1/2 cup Irish Mist
1/4 cup butter (or margarine),
  melted
Salt

In large skillet cook sausage until crumbly. Drain. Mix in bread crumbs, ¼ cup Irish Mist and apple. Set aside.

Brush cut edges of squash with mixture of butter and remaining Irish Mist; spoon remainder into squash cavities. Fill with stuffing mixture.

Place in shallow baking dish. Pour 1 inch water around squash. Cover and bake in 375° oven 45-60 minutes or until squash is tender. Serves 4.

VIKING STEW

1 lb. venison or stew beef,
  cut into 1" cubes
2 tbsps. flour
1½ tsp. salt
1/4 tsp. pepper
2 tbsps. butter (or margarine)
1 medium onion, sliced
1 large carrot, sliced
1 medium stalk celery,
  thinly sliced
Dash each mace and nutmeg
1 tbsp. finely minced parsley
1/2 cup Irish Mist
1½ cups water
1 tbsp. red wine vinegar
1 medium tomato, diced
6 baked patty shells

Coat meat with flour, seasoned with salt and pepper. In large skillet brown meat well in butter.

Mix in remaining ingredients except tomato and patty shells. Simmer 1½ hours or until meat is tender.

Stir in tomato and heat through.

Spoon into patty shells. Serves 6.

DESSERTS

CINAMMON APPLES

4 baking apples, cored
1/2 cup brown sugar
1 tsp. cinnamon
1/4 tsp. nutmeg
1/4 cup roasted, blanched
  slivered almonds
1/4 cup seedless raisins
1/4 cup Irish Mist
3/4 cup water
juice of one lemon
1/4 tsp. finely grated orange rind

Peel 1″ from top of each apple. Place apples in 2 quart baking dish. Mix brown sugar, cinnamon, nutmeg, almonds, and raisins. Fill center of each apple with mixture.

Mix Irish Mist, water, lemon juice, and orange rind. Pour over apples.

Bake in preheated 350° oven 35-40 minutes or until apples are tender. Serve apples in individual dishes. Spoon sauce over apples. Serves 4.

BANANA-PINEAPPLE FLAMBE

3 tbsps. each butter
  (or margarine) and brown
  sugar
2 tbsps. sugar
1/2 cup drained pineapple
  chunks
2 bananas, sliced
1/2 cup Irish Mist
1 qt. vanilla ice cream

Melt butter in skillet or shallow crepe pan over direct heat. Mix in sugars.

Add pineapple and bananas and turn to coat in syrup. Heat until bubbly.

Add Irish Mist. Ignite carefully. Serve hot over vanilla ice cream. Serves 4-6.

VALHALLA

1 package (3 oz.) lady fingers,
  split
1 package (3½-3¾ oz.) instant
  vanilla pudding
1¼ cups milk
1/4 cup Irish Mist
1 cup (½ pint) heavy cream
1 tbsp. confectioners' sugar
1 tbsp. finely minced crystallized ginger

Line 1 quart serving dish with lady fingers. Set aside.

In large mixing bowl, blend together pudding mix, milk, Irish Mist and ½ cup heavy cream. Beat 2-3 minutes or until thickened. Pour into lined serving dish.

Beat remaining cream and sugar until stiff. Fold in ginger. Spread over pudding mixture.

Chill several hours or overnight. Serves 8.

AFTER DINNER DRINKS

On the rocks
Straight

IRISH MIST COFFEE

1 generous cup of steaming coffee
1½ oz. Irish Mist
Top with whipped cream.

MORE WHISKEY LIQUEURS

Irish Mist is made with the purest Irish whiskey. Some very fine liqueurs are made on the same principles, but with Scotch or American whiskies instead.

Drambuie, the best known liqueur from Scotland, is made of fine Scotch whiskey and heather honey, herbs and spices with a slightly smokey taste. Drambuie, the Gaelic word for the "drink that satisfies" is associated with one of the most famous episodes of Scottish history. After the battle of Culloden in 1746, the Scottish rebels were defeated and Bonnie Prince Charlie (Prince Charles Edward Stuart) became a hunted man. Mac Kinnon, one of his followers, gave him shelter and helped him to escape to France. As a token of his gratitude, Bonnie Prince Charlie gave Mac Kinnon the recipe for this fine drink. The Mac Kinnon family still produces this liqueur. In case you have always wondered what a "Rusty Nail" would taste like:

> *1-1/2 oz, Drambuie*
> *1-1/2 oz. Scotch*

Combine, add ice and stir gently.

Glen Mist, is a more recent liqueur, it tastes of spices, and honey, with maybe a hint of a citrus fruit.

Holy Isle, as Drambuie, is rich in Scottisch lore. In 634 A.D. St. Adrian came to the Holy Island of Lindisfarne off the Northumbrian coast. He introduced the local Scottish population to the Christian faith and to the strong drink. It is a light liqueur with a clean taste. If you can't wear it, why not try to taste a "Monk's habit" from the Holy Isle.

> *Place 4 small ice cubes in an old fashioned glass. Add 3/4 oz.*
> *of Holy Isle liqueur. Squeeze 1/2 inch wedge of fresh lemon into*
> *glass. Put lemon, orange slice and cocktail cherry on a toothpick*
> *and muddle the fruit by pressing with the back of a spoon.*
> *Add a 1/4 oz. of water. A final stir.*

Lochan Ora has the privilege to be made with Chivas Regal Scotch.

Usquaebach, "The Grand Liqueur Whisky of the Highlands" is made with one of the oldest Scotch whiskies known, first created under the reign of Mary, Queen of Scots.

Some very fine liqueurs are also based not on Irish or Scotch whisky but on American whisky, *bourbon.*

Wild Turkey Liqueur "the perfect finish to any meal," comes from Kentucky.

Southern Comfort.   The story goes that a distinguished gentleman in the days of Old New Orleans did not care for the taste of even the finest whiskeys of the time. As a result he mixed rare and delicious ingredients (bourbon, oranges, peaches) to create his own liqueur. Southern Comfort is tasty straight, on the rocks or in cocktails such as the "Southern Comfort Collins,"

1-1/2 oz. Southern Comfort
the juice of a 1/4 lime and Seven-Up.

Mix Southern Comfort and lime juice in a tall glass. Add ice cubes, fill with Seven-Up.

And here is a very popular liqueur made with rye

Rock and Rye.   A lovely amber colored American liqueur. Originally it was made of a combination of rye whiskey, rock candy, lemon and orange juices. Today's product frequently combines cherries and other fruits. It tastes very good indeed and is considered *the* remedy for colds. If you are sneezing, coughing, sniffling and wheezing, try:

A most comforting Toddy

Put one clove, a bit of a cinnamon stick and a lemon twist in a mug.
Add a generous jigger of Rock and Rye. Fill with boiling water.
Drink, and sweet dreams.

A Taste of Mint

CREME DE MENTHE

Mint is a fragrant and refreshing herb. There are no superstitions or magic qualities attached to it. It is easily grown and has been universally used for centuries. The Egyptians were quite fond of mint as a digestive and cooling plant. The Greeks added it to their bath water much as we add softening ingredients to our own. It symbolizes virtue, probably because of its cleansing properties. The popularity of mint has never decreased, the Arabs brew it with tea. Mint Julep was the favorite drink of the Old South, The Temperance League in the 30's considered mint as an incentive to drinking and wanted to uproot the mint beds.

Crème de menthe is distilled from mint leaves. The precise flavor of each brand of crème de menthe varies according to the type of mint leaves used to produce it. For instance, in France, Get Frères, the most popular manufacturers of menthe liqueur, have been using five different mints from five different countries for two hundred years: England, France, Russia, Bulgaria and Morocco. Other manufacturers believe that the mint beds found in Croydon, England, are the best in the world. Oregon also has an excellent reputation for its mint.

There is a lovely legend attached to the name "mint": Pluto fell in love with a nymph named Mintha. In Greek mythology, husbands were often unfaithful and wives jealous and revengeful. This was no exception. Pluto's wife, Prosperpine, metamorphosed the nymph into the herb named after her. Aren't we lucky!

CREME DE MENTHE

DRINKS

Stinger:

2 oz. brandy
1 oz. crème de menthe (white)
Shake with cracked ice. Strain into frosted cocktail glass.

Mint Julep:

1 oz. crème de menthe (green)
2 oz. bourbon
Stir well, pour over ice cubes. Garnish with fresh mint leaves.
If you feel like a long drink add soda water.

Grasshopper:

1 oz. crème de menthe (green)
1 oz. creme de cacao (white)
1 oz. cream
Shake with cracked ice. Strain into frosted cocktail glass.

Prosperpine's Revenge:

1½ oz. crème de menthe (white)
1 oz. cognac
Pour in the crème de menthe, add slowly cognac on top so
that it floats on the surface. Serve with short straw.

Irish Clover:

1/2 oz. crème de menthe (green)
1/2 dry vermouth
1½ oz. Irish whisky
Shake with cracked ice. Strain into a chilled glass.

Rum and Crème de Menthe:

1 oz. crème de menthe (green)
2 oz. light rum
1 tbsp. lime juice
Shake on ice and strain into chilled cocktail glass.

ENTREES

LAMB CHOPS A LA MENTHE

6 loin chops
2 tbsps. teriyaki sauce
salt and pepper to taste
1/4 cup crème de menthe (green)

Heat one tablespoon of each butter and oil in a large frying pan.

Brown chops 5 minutes on each side. Pour off the fat. Remove chops to a hot platter. Add teriyaki sauce and crème de menthe. Stir well and pour over chops. Serve immediately on warm plates (lamb should be eaten while it's hot). Makes 3 to 6 servings according to your appetite and the abundance of side dishes.

LEG OF LAMB WITH A MINT GLAZE

1-6 to 8 lbs leg of lamb
1 tbsp mustard
1 tbsp olive oil (or vegetable oil)
1/2 cup crème de menthe (white)
3 cloves garlic (optional)

Preheat oven to 325°. For garlic lovers: with a sharp knife, make 3 cuts in the leg of lamb and insert garlic cloves. If the taste of garlic offends you, proceed to the next step: mix mustard, oil and crème de menthe. Brush lamb with mixture. Baste frequently with pan juices. Roast 25 minutes per pound for medium rare.

ARTICHOKES VINAIGRETTE

4 cooked artichokes
8 tbsps. olive oil (or salad oil)
3 tbsps. vinegar
Salt and pepper to taste
2 tbsps. white crème de menthe
Mix well. Enjoy!

Dip artichoke leaves in the vinaigrette.
"I love you, I love you not"

MINTED NEW PEAS

Cook fresh peas with mint leaves. When peas are tender, drain, add
2 tbsps. of butter and 1 tbsp. of green crème de menthe.

DESSERTS

QUICK CREME DE MENTHE FRAPPE

1 package (3 oz.) lemon
   or lime gelatin
3/4 cup boiling water
1½ cups crushed ice
2 tbsps. crème de menthe
   liqueur

Combine gelatin and boiling water in
blender. Cover and blend at low speed
until the gelatin is dissolved. Add
crushed ice and crème de menthe.
Blend at high speed until the ice is
melted. Pour into 4-cup ring mold.
Chill at least 30 minutes. Unmold.
Serves 4 to 6.

DUTCH MINT

1 oz. green crème de menthe
4 oz. chocolate ice-cream.

Spin in blender until smooth. Serve in
cocktail glass. Top with chocolate
chips. Serves 6.

STARS AND STRIPES

1 pint vanilla ice-cream
2 oz. green crème de menthe
2 oz. brown crème de cacao

Take out 2 parfait glasses. Pour 1/2 oz. crème de menthe in the bottom of each glass. Spoon in some ice-cream. Now add 1/2 oz. crème de cacao, then spoon in some ice-cream and go on alternating crème de menthe, ice-cream and crème de cacao until glass is full. Put in freezer until serving time (this dessert can be prepared ahead of time) Serves 2.

Crème de menthe (green) is delicious over grapefruit.

FRUIT TOPPING

3/4 cup sour cream
1 tbsp. green crème de menthe
1 tbsp. crème de cacao (brown)
  or white)
1 tbsp. light brown sugar

Combine ingredients and chill. A pleasant topping for fresh fruits, particularly blueberries.

AFTER DINNER DRINKS

1 oz. green crème de menthe
1 oz. white crème de menthe
  Serve in chilled glasses.

Green crème de menthe frappé
Pour a dash of white creme de menthe in your coffee.

All mint liqueurs are not crèmes de menthe. If you enjoy a drier cordial with a more definite peppermint taste, try Peppermint Schnapps (this liqueur bears no relation to the "schnapps" served in Holland and Germany).

PEPPERMINT SCHNAPPS ALEXANDER

1½ oz. Peppermint Schnapps
1½ oz. gin
3/4 oz. cream

Shake over ice. Strain into a chilled cocktail glass.

PEPPERMINT SCHNAPPS STINGER

1 oz. Peppermint Schnapps
1¾ oz. brandy or cognac

Shake over ice. Strain into chilled cocktail glass. For a drier Stinger, use a little less Schnapps.

MORE ABOUT HERBS AND PLANTS

There are not yet as many tea-flavored liqueurs as coffee. But tea-lovers can choose from:

Aqua Turco Liqueur: green Chinese tea, gun-powder tea, vanilla essence, sugar syrup, musk on a wine and spirit base.
Marmot Tea: a delicately flavored liqueur from Switzerland. Delicious straight or in hot tea.
Ocha: A pleasant green Japanese cordial. It is a fine after dinner drink and delicious over ice-cream.
Suntory Green Tea Liqueur: made from two traditional Japanese teas, Matcha and Gyokura, blended for a unique oriental flavor.
Tiffin: made with Darjeeling tea, a perfect companion for iced tea.

Some liqueurs and cordials are made with the flowers or petals of plants; think of a garden in the spring and of sweet smells, and try:

Crème de Rose: neutral spirit, aromatized seeds, colored and flavored with sweetened rose petals.

Rosolio: this liqueur is quite popular in Italy and Turkey. It is made from petals of red roses, "eau de fleur d'oranger" (orange blossom water), jasmine, cinnamon, clove, neutral spirit and a varying amount of sugar according to the manufacturers.

Crème de violet: the same as crème de rose, but fresh violets are used instead of rose petals.

Crème Yvette: This is an all American cordial. It tastes of fresh violets and vanilla.

Violets cordials are particularly romantic since violets symbolize faithfulness and love. Shakespeare believed that Ophelia's soul would bloom again as a violet:

> *Lay her in the earth*
> *And from her fair and unpolluted flesh*
> *May violets spring.*
> *Hamlet, Act V, scene I*

Some cordials are made with the roots of plants like licorice which we discuss with anise tasting liqueurs, and ginger.

Ginger flavored brandy: For a different flavor try:

Ginger flavored brandy and ginger ale.

Ginger flavored brandy on crushed ice, or 2 oz. vodka and 1 oz. ginger flavored brandy on the rocks.

CHICKEN LIVERS WITH AN ORIENTAL TASTE

1 ½ lb. chicken livers
1 large clove garlic minced
1/4 cup each oil and Teriyaki
  sauce ·
1 can (8 oz.) water chestnuts
1 can (8 oz.) straw mushrooms
  (available in Chinese grocery
  stores)
4 slices bacon
1 large onion, sliced
1/2 cup ginger flavored brandy

In a large bowl, combine chicken livers, ginger brandy, oil, Teriyaki sauce, garlic and water chestnuts. Cover. Refrigerate for several hours, stirring occasionally. Then, cook bacon in a large skillet until crisp. Remove bacon, crumble and reserve.

To drippings in the pan, add onion, drained chicken livers, water chestnuts and straw mushrooms. Cook stirring until livers are done to your taste. Sprinkle bacon on top. Serve with rice or alone. Serves 4.

Finish the meal with ginger flavored brandy over oranges, grapefruit, peaches or baked apples.

A TASTE OF COFFEE

KALHUA FROM MEXICO

Kalhúa is made with an ingredient particularly rich in legend: coffee. In ancient Ethiopia, Kaldi, a young goat herder, saw his goats skipping and dancing in the sun one day. The boy was astonished; he looked around and discovered that they were eating the red berries of a wild shrub. He hurried to the neighboring monastery. The whole thing seemed like magic or witchcraft to him. The abbott decided to come out and observe for himself the strange behavior of the goats. Then he picked some of those strange berries, brewed them and served the new beverage to his monks. The result was magical! Instead of falling asleep over the long night services, they stayed awake!

We still don't know how coffee became the favorite drink of the Near East, but we know that the first coffee house was established in Constantinople in the middle of the XVIth century. It created a controversy: the very orthodox Muslims declared that coffee was intoxicating and therefore prohibited by the Koran.

It took a while for coffee to come to Europe, but when it did, its popularity was immediate and it has never diminished since. When the first coffee house opened in Saint Michael's Alley in Oxford, people came in throngs to taste this new, invigorating drink which stimulated the mind and added an unusual spark to social encounters. The coffee houses in England became centers of wit and culture and were nicknamed "penny universities" because a cup of coffee sold for a penny. Little by little, they turned into exclusive clubs. On the continent and particularly in France, they developed into the simple "café." In France, the first coffee house appeared in Marseille in 1671, which at the time was one of the foremost trading centers with the East. Paris followed suit a few years later and all through the XVIIIth century coffee houses were important centers of political, philosophical and literary life. Diderot and Rousseau used to meet their friends there and endlessly discuss the problems of their day.

The first American coffee house opened in Boston in 1670 and coffee soon became an important part of American life. The Merchant coffee house in New York and the Green Dragon in Boston played an important part in national affairs as a favorite political meeting place.

People of the Middle East controlled the production of coffee until the beginning of the XVIIth century. Then the Dutch started growing it in their Javanese territories and in Ceylon. The English did the same in the West Indies. Then the cultivation of coffee spread to Brazil, Mexico, Hawaii and finally to Africa.

KALHUA

DRINKS

Kalhúa and club soda

Kalhúa and scotch
1 oz. Kalhúa
2 oz. scotch
Mix well and serve on the rocks.

Black Russian
1 oz. Kalhúa
2 oz. vodka
Mix well and serve on the rocks.

ENTREES

CHICKEN LIVERS KALHUA

2 tbsps. butter or margarine
1 large onion, sliced
1/2 green pepper, diced
2 cloves garlic minced
3 oz. ham, cut into strips
Juice of half a lemon
1/4 cup parsley, chopped
1 teaspoon basil crushed
1 teaspoon oregano, crushed
1/2 cup Kalhúa
2 tbsps. brandy
1½ lb chicken livers
10 medium sized mushrooms
  sliced
Salt and pepper to taste

In a large skillet, melt the butter or margarine, and saute onion, green pepper, garlic and ham until soft. Stir in lemon juice, basil, oregano, parsley and Kalhúa. Simmer for 5 minutes. Add chicken livers and mushrooms. Turn livers often so that they brown on all sides. Season with salt and pepper. Serve with rice or buttered noodles. Serves 4.

FILET MIGNON KALHUA

4 slices filet mignon (1½ lb.)
2 tbsp butter or margarine
1/2 cup Kalhúa
1 large clove garlic, minced
1 jar Bearnaise sauce (6 oz.)
1 tbsp lemon juice
1 tbsp chopped parsley
3/4 lb. mushrooms, sliced
Salt and pepper to taste

Melt butter in a large skillet, cook the filets according to taste. Pour ¼ cup Kalhúa and brandy over them and flambe. When the flames have died, remove the filets to a heated covered platter. Add garlic and mushrooms to the pan. Cook until soft. Add the remaining Kalhúa, Béarnaise sauce and lemon juice. Heat but do not boil. Pour over steaks, garnish with parsley and serve at once. Serves 4.

You can substitute boneless sirlon steaks for filet mignon if your budget needs to be stretched.

DESSERTS

KALHUA MOUSSE

1½ cups of milk
1 envelope unflavored gelatin
1/2 cup Kalhúa
1 egg
1/4 cup sugar
1/8 tsp. salt
6 oz. semi-sweet chocolate
  chips
1 cup heavy cream

Heat milk and gelatin in a small saucepan to boiling point, stirring constantly to dissolve gelatin. Pour into a blender with all the other ingredients except cream. Blend at medium speed until smooth. Add cream, blend at low speed. until well blended. Pour into a mold. Chill for several hours. Serves 8.

KALHUA ICE CREAM

1 quart heavy cream
1 cup light cream
3/4 cup sugar
1 tsp. vanilla extract
5 oz. Kalhúa
2 tbsps. instant coffee

Combine all ingredients, add a pinch of salt. Put in a freezer container and freeze overnight or longer. Serves 6-8.

Kalhúa is delicious over vanilla ice-cream, or coffee ice-cream or chocolate ice-cream, or on a mixture of the three.

AFTER DINNER DRINKS

Straight or on the rocks

Sombrero:

1-½ oz Kalhúa
1-½ oz milk
Shake with crushed ice, strain into a brandy snifter.

Sweet volcano:

1 tbsp Kalhúa in hot strong coffee sugared to taste, top with whipped cream.

Cortés:

1 oz Kalhúa
1 oz light rum
dash of lemon juice

Serve over cracked ice in brandy snifter.

TIA MARIA FROM JAMAICA

Liqueur recipes are as closely guarded as defense secrets. However the adventures of a "liqueur spy" have yet to be written! This much is known about Tia Maria: it is made from the essence of the richest coffee beans and blended exotic spices from the famous island.

Stories are beautiful but even the most extraordinary fairy tales are sometimes better untold. Today, only warm ocean breezes are left to whisper the many legends surrounding Tia Maria's origins.

Even so, the exotic liqueur will recreate an atmosphere in your home as romantic and exciting as the island it comes from.

DRINKS

On the rocks.

Tia 'N Soda

Tia Maria
Juice of ¼ lemon
Club soda
Pour generous dollop of Tia Maria into highball glass, add lemon juice, fill with club soda, decorate with lemon slice and mint leaves.

Cappuccino Cocktail

1 part Tia Maria
1 part vodka
1 part fresh cream
Shake with cracked ice, strain into cocktail glass.

Black Pearl

1 part Tia Maria
1 part cognac
Champagne
Chill a large champagne glass, pour in Tia Maria and cognac and fill to brim with champagne. Garnish with black cherry.

Eight Ball

1 part Tia Maria
1 part vodka
Stir with ice, strain into cocktail glass.

Moon Walker

1 part Tia Maria
1 dash bitters
3 parts blended whiskey
1 maraschino cherry
Stir well with ice, strain into cocktail glass, add cherry.

The Limbo

1 part Tia Maria
1 part gin
Stir gently, chill and serve in cocktail glass. if desired, garnish with twist of lemon.

ENTREES

JAMAICAN ASPARAGUS SOUP

32 oz. canned asparagus soup
8 oz. cooked asparagus (fresh or canned)
4 oz. Tia Maria

Pour soup in saucepan. Add asparagus and Tia Maria. Serve piping hot. Serves 4.

TIA MARIA SHRIMP DIP

1 lb. shrimps, shelled, chopped
1 lb. shrimps, shelled for
  garnish
1/2 lb. cold pasta or cooked
  diced potatoes
1/2 cup mayonnaise
1 cup chopped celery
2 oz. Tia Maria
salt & pepper (to taste)

Mix all ingredients in a large bowl and chill.

Decorate by surrounding rim of bowl with a frieze of shrimps. Serve with black and white breads cut into intriguing shapes with cookie cutter, and long French bread, slit lengthwise, scooped out and heated. Serves 6-8.

BARBECUED HAM STEAKS

3 one-inch ham steaks
2 cups Tia Maria
1/4 cup dry mustard
1/4 cup melted butter
1/4 cup brown sugar
1 minced garlic
clove
1/2 tablespoon paprika

Marinate ham steaks at room temperature for two hours in combined Tia Maria, butter, mustard, brown sugar, garlic and paprika. Turn steaks once or twice and baste with marinade. Broil for 10 minutes on each side, basting frequently with the marinade. Serves 6.

DESSERTS

CHOCOLATE SOUFFLE TIA MARIA

3 tbsp butter
3 tbsp flour
1 cup milk
1/2 cup sugar
2 squares unsweetened
  chocolate, melted
1 tsp vanilla
1/2 cup Tia Maria
4 egg yolks
5 egg whites

Butter 1½ qt. souffle dish or casserole and sprinkle with sugar until coated. Melt butter in a saucepan. Blend in flour. Gradually add milk, stirring constantly. Mix in sugar, salt, chocolate and vanilla and cook over low heat until thick and smooth. Remove from heat: add Tia Maria. Beat egg yolks lightly and add to chocolate mixture. Beat egg whites until stiff and fold into yolk mixture. Pour into souffle dish. Place dish in pan of hot, *not boiling* water and bake in 400⁰ oven 15 minutes. Reduce heat to 375⁰ and bake 20 to 25 minutes longer or until knife inserted in center comes out clean. Serve immediately with whipped cream or a sauce. Serves 6.

TIA MARIE PIE SURPRISE

Add ¼ cup Tia Maria to your favorite chocolate or butterscotch pie filling or package mix. Add the same amount to a chocolate or butterscotch pudding. Top with cup of whipped cream to which 2 tablespoons of Tia Maria have been added.

AFTER DINNER DRINKS

Tia Maria Cream

1/3 Tia Maria
1/3 heavy cream
1/3 coffee or espresso
Shake with ice strain and serve in whiskey sour glass.

Jamaican Coffee

Pour a generous dollop of Tia Maria into hot black coffee, top with whipped cream.

Tia Rumba

1 part Tia Maria
1 part rum
Stir gently, chill briefly and serve in cocktail glass.

Limbo Cow

1 part Tia Maria
2 parts milk
Serve on the rocks in old-fashioned glass.

MORE ABOUT COFFEE

Americans love the taste of coffee. Coffee flavored cordials are very popular in this country and as diversified as the varieties of coffee beans.

Coffee liqueurs are most enjoyable in coffee, in frappés, in ice-cold milk with ice cubes, and over ice-cream.

AUSTRIA	**Old Vienna coffee Liqueur**
BRAZIL.	**Bahia**
IRELAND.	**Galway's Irish Coffee Liqueur**
ITALY.	**Espresso**
SWITZERLAND	**Marmot Mocca**

A Taste of Chocolate

CREME DE CACAO

Centuries before the Spanish conquest, Indians had cultivated the cocoa tree from Southern Mexico to Northern South America. Cocoa was called "cacahuate" or "chocoate" in Maya dialect. When Cortez arrived in the Aztec Empire, Montezuma offered him a chocolate drink and he loved it. The Spanish and the Portuguese began to grow cocoa trees all through their territories. It was soon introduced in some of the Caribbean Islands, then in the Gulf of Guinea and later to Africa and the Far East.

When Columbus came back from one of his voyages to the New World, he was quick to call the possibilities of cocoa to the attention of King Ferdinand of Spain.

Early in the XVIIth century, the brother of the French cardinal de Richelieu brought the cocoa bean to France where for a long time it was considered a highly valued luxury product. The other ingredient often found in a crème of cocoa, vanilla, is not a bean but a member of the orchid family. It is also a native of South America that was introduced in Europe by the conquistadors. Vanilla was soon enjoyed widely and later was used to flavor food and tobacco and even perfumes. Cocoa beans are roasted, crushed, and macerated in spirits. Small quantities of vanilla enhance the subtle chocolate flavor.

DRINKS

Brandy Alexander:
1 oz. brandy
1 oz. crème de cacao
1 oz. cream
Shake with cracked ice, strain into a cocktail glass.

A West Indian Surprise:
1 oz. brown crème de cacao
1 oz. dark rum
2 oz. frozen pineapple juice concentrate
Mix pineapple juice with the shaved ice in a 4 oz. glass. Add crème de cacao and rum. Stir and serve with a short straw.

The Grasshopper:
1 oz. green crème de menthe
1 oz. white crème de cacao
1 oz. cream
Shake with cracked ice and strain into a cocktail glass.

ENTREE

OLE CHICKEN MOLE

1 chicken, 3½ lbs.
2 tablespoons oil
1/4 cup blanched almonds
1 tablespoon toasted sesame
  seeds
1 square (1 oz.) unsweetened
  chocolate
1 slice toasted bread
1 can (1 lb. 12 oz.) tomatoes
  packed in puree
4 teaspoons chili powder
2 teaspoons salt
1/2 teaspoon ground cumin
1/4 teaspoon cinnamon
1/4 teaspoon pepper
1 clove garlic
3 oz. Régnier crème de Cacao
  (brown)
4 cups hot cooked rice

Cut chicken into serving pieces. Heat in oil in a Dutch oven and brown chicken on all sides. Remove from pan. Put almonds, sesame seeds, chocolate and toast into jar of blender and chop finely; or use finest blade of a food chopper. Put the nut and spice mixture into pan. Add tomatoes, seasonings, and garlic. Bring sauce to a boil, stirring constantly. Reduce the heat, simmer 15 minutes, stirring often. Return chicken to pan; baste with sauce. Cover, bake in a pre-heated 350⁰ oven 45 minutes, or until chicken is tender. Add crème de Cacao; baste, bake 5 minutes longer. Serve with hot rice. Serves 6.

GRASSHOPPER PIE

14 hydrox cookies
2 tbsps. butter
24 marshmallows
1/2 cup milk
4 tbsps. green creme de menthe
2 tbsps. white creme de cacao
1 cup whipped cream

Crush 14 hydrox cookies, stir in 2 tablespoons melted butter. Press the mixture into an 8 inch pie plate. Melt 24 marshmallows in ½ cup milk. Cool for 30 minutes. Stir in 4 tbsps. green creme de menthe and 3 tbsps. white creme de cacao. Fold in a cup whipped cream, pour into pie shell Freeze and serve frozen. Sprinkle the top with chocolate chips. Serves 6.

SPECIAL ICE-CREAM COMBINATION

In parfait glasses, alternate layers of vanilla ice-cream and brown crème de cacao, starting and ending with the liqueur. Optional: top the dessert with whipped cream.

You can also use brown crème de cacao and green creme de menthe. This dessert can be made just before serving, or prepared ahead of time, frozen and served frozen.

CREME DE CACAO CAKE

1 prepared chocolate cake mix
  (choose your favorite)
6 oz. brown crème de cacao

Prepare the cake according to directions. Substitute 3 oz. crème de cacao for 3 oz. of the liquid called for in the directions. If you plan to frost the cake, again substitute 3 oz. crème de cacao for 3 oz. of the liquid required for the frosting.

POIRES DE CACAO

1 large can of pears
1/2 cup liquid from the can
1/2 brown crème de cacao

Drain the pears. Mix liquid from the can and creme de cacao.

Pour over pears and chill for 4 to 5 hours. Before serving, top the dessert with whipped cream and sprinkle with instant coffee.

AFTER DINNER DRINKS

Crème de cacao white or brown or straight or on the rocks.

Angel's tip:

1 oz. crème de cacao (brown)
1 tbsp. heavy cream

Float heavy cream on top. Add a cherry. A tip: pour the cream gently over the back of the spoon.

Mexican Coffee:

1 cup of hot, strong coffee
Sugar to taste
A dash of ground cloves
1 oz. brown crème de cacao
Cinnamon Stick

Put sugar and cloves in coffee, stir, add crème de cacao. Serve with a cinnamon stick for stirring.

MORE ABOUT CHOCOLATE

Chocolate can compete with tea and coffee for popularity. Every cordial house has at least one or two chocolate flavored liqueurs besides crème de cacao.

Marmot au Chocolat: This liqueur from Switzerland is a distilled product with chocolate chips floating in it.

Vandermint was one of the first and still is one of the most popular chocolate-mint liqueurs. It comes from Holland. Try
1 oz. Vandermint
1 oz. crème de menthe (white)
Stir well and serve over shaved ice.

or *1 oz. Vandermint*
1 oz. crème de café
Stir well and serve over shaved ice.

or *1 oz. Vandermint*
1 oz. brandy
Stir well and serve over shaped ice.

Chocolate mixes very well with fruits. One of the best known combinations is Cheri-Suisse (chocolate and cherries):

Cheri-Suisse Kiss:

1 oz. vodka
4 to 5 oz. orange juice over ice in an 8 oz. glass.
Top with 1/2 oz. Cheri-Suisse.

Cheri-Suisse Alexander:

1 oz. Cheri-Suisse
1 oz. gin
1 oz. cream
Shake with cracked ice. Strain into a cocktail glass.

or for a very special occasion try the glory of

Cheri-Jubilee:

1 jar (14-16 oz.) pitted dark sweet cherries
1 tablespoon sugar
2 teaspoons cornstarch
1 oz. Cheri-Suisse
12 scoops vanilla ice-cream
For flambé:
1 oz. Cheri-Suisse
1 oz. rum

Drain the cherries. Pour the syrup into a sauce pan or chafing dish.
Stir in 1 tablespoon sugar and 2 teaspoons cornstarch. Heat, stirring
until thickened.

Add cherries and 1 oz. Cheri-Suisse. Keep the sauce warm and dish out
the ice-cream. Then, combine Cheri-Suisse and rum. Warm: ignite
and pour into pan. Spoon flaming sauce and cherries over ice-cream.
Serves 6.

For a taste of the tropics, try **Choclair** (chocolate and coconut).

Wooden Shoe:

2 oz. Choclair
1 oz. vodka

Serve over ice.

Creamy Fruit Dessert:

2 large bananas, sliced
1 cup (8 oz.) sour cream
1/4 cup diced fresh oranges
1/4 teaspoon vanilla extract
1/3 cup Choclair

Fold all ingredients together. Serve in individual sherbet glasses. Chill
several hours. Garnish with mint sprigs and curls of orange peels.
Serves 4.

But it is also easy to become fond of:

Chocolate-banana

Chocolate-raspberry

Chocolate-orange (for example *Sabra,* the liqueur from Israel) and

Chocolate-Amaretto which seems to have captured cordial houses' fancy.

Banana Split, Italian style

A Taste of Almonds

AMARETTO DI SARONNO

In Italian, Amaretto means "a little bitter." It is also a name given to "amaretti," sweets made with local almonds. Although almonds have been added to brandy and alcohol for centuries, Amaretto is not made with almonds but with apricot pits which have a slightly bitter almond flavor.

Maybe it is only a legend, but it is a haunting one. In 1525, Lombardy was ravaged by famine, pestilence and war. Still, a few privileged people managed to escape these horrors. One of them was an obscure artist, who has now become famous, Bernardino Luini. He belonged to the Leonardo Da Vinci school and was painting a fresco in the sanctuary of Santa Maria della Grazie in Saronno, a hamlet near Milano. Meanwhile, he was living in a nearby inn. The innkeeper was young, beautiful, blonde and widowed. She is now immortalized as the Madonna in the Chapel of the Sanctuary. She was very poor—she had two small children to raise—but she wanted to express her gratitude to the painter. So she invented a special drink for Luini: almonds from apricot pits, which as the legend goes, her daughter gathered, and alcohol combined with other unknown ingredients. We would like to think it was the beginning of a love story. Successive innkeepers continued to serve this drink. In 1800, Carlo Dominico Reina succeeded in obtaining the formula for Amaretto. He then sold it in his apothecary shop. Since 1939, Amaretto has been produced commercially.

Neutral alcohol, apricot pits, aromatic herbs (it would be nice to know which ones, but it's a well kept secret) contribute to give Amaretto its rich, fruity, satisfying nutty taste.

DRINKS

On the rocks
With club soda

Rum Amaretto:

1 oz. Amaretto di Saronno
1 oz. light rum
Pour over shaved ice and add a splash of club soda if desired.

Bourbon Amaretto:

1½ oz. of your favorite bourbon
3/4 oz. Amaretto di Saronno
Serve on the rocks.

ENTREES

PEACH CONSERVE

Prepare on a rainy day, when everything else fails. Serve with pork, ham and curry dishes.

4 lbs. fresh peaches, peeled, pitted and diced.
48 dried apricot halves, cut in small pieces
3 cups light brown sugar
3 cups granulated sugar
1 teaspoon cinnamon
1 cup blanched, toasted almonds, chopped
3/4 cup Amaretto di Saronno

Combine first 5 ingredients and cook over high heat about 15 minutes or until mixture is thickened, stirring occasionally. Remove from heat and stir in remaining ingredients. Pour into hot sterilized glasses and seal. Makes eight 8-oz. glasses.

SPICY CRANBERRY SAUCE

Serve with Thanksgiving or Christmas turkey.

1 cup water
1 cup sugar
1/2 teaspoon ginger
1 hard pear, peeled and diced
2 cups cranberries
1 lemon (grated rind, plus juice)
1/4 cup Amaretto di Saronno

Combine water, sugar, ginger: boil 5 minutes. Add pear, simmer for 3 minutes. Add cranberries and continue cooking sauce, without stirring, until the cranberries pop open. Cool the sauce. Just before serving, stir in lemon juice, rind and Amaretto. Serve in relish dish to accompany turkey.

VEAL A L'ORANGE REINA

6 veal cutlets, pounded very thin and seasoned with salt and pepper
1/4 cup butter
2 tablespoons finely chopped shallots
Juice of 1 lemon and 1 orange
1/4 cup Amaretto di Saronno
2 teaspoons each: lemon and orange peel
1 cup milk
2 tablespoons flour
1 cup chicken stock
1 can (8 oz.) mushrooms
1/4 cup sour cream
Salt and pepper to taste

Saute the cutlets in the butter in a skillet until lightly browned. Put the cutlets in a shallow baking dish, cover and bake at 300° for 20 minutes.

Cook shallots in the juices in the skillet until soft. Stir in next 5 ingredients and simmer, stirring to loosen brown bits from the bottom of the skillet. Mix milk and flour and add to pan. Cook, stirring until the sauce is thickened and smooth. Add stock and mushrooms and simmer a minute or two more. Remove from heat and stir in sour cream. Add salt and pepper and pour sauce over cutlets. Serves 6.

CARROTS DEL TURCO

1 pound carrots, grated
3/4 cup water
1/2 teaspoon salt
1/4 teaspoon sugar
1/4 cup butter
2 tablespoons slivered almonds
2 tablespoons Amaretto di
  Saronno
1 teaspoon lemon juice
Salt and pepper to taste

Put first 4 ingredients in a skillet, bring to a boil, cover and cook over low heat for 10 minutes, stirring occasionally and watching that carrots do not burn (add more water if necessary).

Combine remaining ingredients, heat gently and stir into carrots just before serving. Serves 4 to 6.

ROAST PORK SARONNO

3 pound loin of pork roast
1 can (8 oz.) tomato sauce
1/2 cup catsup
1/2 cup vinegar
1/2 cup brown sugar
1/2 cup dark corn syrup
1/2 teaspoon chili powder
1 tablespoon cornstarch
4 tablespoons Amaretto di
  Saronno

Roast the pork in the usual manner. Combine next 7 ingredients and cook over low heat 5 min. Blend cornstarch with 2 tbsps. of the mixture and add it to the rest, stirring until slightly thickened. Stir in Amaretto and cook 10 to 15 min. Half an hour before the roast is done, remove pan drippings and cover meat with 1/3 of the sauce. Roast 15 min. and add another 1/3 of the sauce. Serve remaining sauce with the roast. Serves 6.

MASHED SWEET POTATOES

6 large sweet potatoes
1/2 stick butter
1½ ounces Amaretto di
  Saronno
1½ ounces cream (if needed
  for softer consistency)

Peel hot cooked sweet potatoes and mash. Gradually adding remaining ingredients, beat until potatoes are fluffy. Garnish with slivered almonds, if desired. Serves 6 to 8.

DESSERTS:

Quick Desserts

STRAWBERRIES ALLA AMARETTO

1 quart washed strawberries
2 tablespoons sugar
1/2 cup Amaretto di Saronno
Vanilla ice cream (optional)

Slice berries, sprinkle with sugar. Pour Amaretto over berries; gently mix and chill. Serve plain or over ice cream. Serves 6.

AMARETTO ZABAIONE

5 egg yolks, plus 1 whole egg
2 tablespoons sugar
1/2 cup Amaretto di
Saronno

Combine egg yolks, egg, sugar in top of double boiler over simmering water. Beat with wire whisk until pale yellow and fluffy. Then, gradually add Amaretto and continue beating until zabaione becomes thick enough to hold its shape in a spoon. This may take as long as 10 minutes.

Spoon into large stemmed glasses and serve while still hot. Serves 4.

Zabaione is delicious by itself or as topping for fruit tarts, fresh fruits, ice cream or combination of both. (See our recipe for Banana Split Italian Style).

More elaborate desserts:

CHOCOLATE FONDUE

3 bars Swiss milk chocolate
  flavored with almonds and
  honey
1/2 cup heavy cream
4 tablespoons Amaretto di
  Saronno
Fresh fruits such as:
  orange sections
  strawberries
  pineapple chunks
  pear sections
Miniature cream puffs
Small pieces of angel food cake
Marshmallows

Break chocolate into pieces. In small chafing dish or saucepan, combine and heat chocolate, cream and Amaretto. Stir over very low heat until chocolate is melted. Serve surrounded by small bowls of fruits and cake. Spear piece of fruit or cake with fondue fork or skewer, dip in warm chocolate mixture. Serves 4.

PUMPKIN MOUSSE

2 tablespoons unflavored
  gelatin
1/2 cup cold water
1/2 cup Amaretto di Saronno
1/2 cup sugar
1 tablespoon lemon juice
1 ½ teaspoons cinnamon
1 teaspoon ginger
2 cups canned pumpkin
1 cup sour cream
1 cup heavy cream, whipped
Chopped walnuts
Additional sweetened whipped
  cream

Soften gelatin in the cold water; place over hot water and dissolve. Add Amaretto, sugar, lemon juice and spices. Stir until well blended and chill untill slightly thickened. Combine pumpkin with sour cream and whipped cream. Combine mixture with slightly thickened gelatin, blending well. Turn mixture into 5-1/2 cup mold and chill until firm. Unmold on chilled platter; garnish with chopped walnuts and sweetened whipped cream. Serves 6 to 8.

BANANA SPLIT, ITALIAN STYLE

6 egg yolks
3 tablespoons sugar
6 tablespoons Amaretto di
  Saronno
6 large bananas
1 pint each strawberry, vanilla
  and pistachio ice cream
Whipped cream, cherries, sliced
  almonds, mixed candied fruits

In the top part of a double boiler, mix egg yolks, sugar and Amaretto di Saronno. Place mixture over hot simmering (not boiling) water and beat with an electric mixer until very thick and creamy, about 7 minutes. Remove from heat and continue beating until mixture is warm. Peel bananas and slice lengthwise and place in serving dishes. Top each banana with 3 scoops of ice cream — strawberry, vanilla and pistachio. Spoon warm Amaretto di Saronno mixture over ice cream. Top with whipped cream, cherries, almonds or candied fruits. Serve at once. Serves 6.

Mocha Cheesecake Saronno

100

MOCHA CHEESECAKE SARONNO

1 cup unsifted all-purpose flour
1/4 cup sugar
Grated rind of 1 lemon
1 egg yolk
1/2 cup cold butter or margarine
5 packages (8 ounces each)
  cream cheese
1½ cups sugar
1/4 cup flour
1/4 teaspoon salt
6 eggs
1/3 cup Amaretto di Saronno
2 tablespoons instant coffee
Sweetened whipped cream

In a bowl, mix flour, sugar and lemon rind. Add egg yolk and butter or margarine; mix with the fingers until a smooth ball of dough is formed. Wrap and chill dough for 1 hour. With floured fingers, pat dough evenly into the bottom and sides of an ungreased 9-inch springform pan. In a bowl, beat cream cheese until fluffy. Gradually beat in sugar, flour and salt. Beat in eggs one at a time, beating well after each addition. Mix Amaretto di Saronno and coffee until coffee is dissolved. Beat this mixture into cheesecake. Pour into dough-lined pan. Bake in a preheated slow oven (250°) for 1½ hours, or until firm when touched in the center. Cool cake and then chill. When ready to serve, remove sides of pan and decorate top of cake with rosettes of sweetened whipped cream or topping. Dust rosettes with additional crushed instant coffee. Cheesecake may be prepared without crust, if preferred. Makes 1 9-inch cheesecake.

AFTER DINNER DRINKS

Amaretto and coffee:

Add 1 oz. of Amaretto di Saronno to hot espresso coffee. Depending on taste, sugar may or may not be added.

Straight or on the rocks.

Amaretto and cognac:

1 oz. Amaretto di Saronno
2 oz. cognac
Serve in snifter.

Amaretto and scotch:

1 oz. Amaretto di Saronno
2 oz. scotch
Serve on the rocks.

MORE ABOUT ALMONDS

Some other interesting liqueurs are made from the kernels or pits of fruits. We have included in this category the nut flavored cremes and cordials.

Crème de Almond, a clear, red cordial, produced by distilling apricot kernels and almonds. It has a very pleasant taste by itself or with vodka.

Crème de noyau; derives its characteristic flavor from kernels or peaches, cherries, plums and apricots. Drink it straight or with vodka.

Crème de noya a cordial made with bitter almonds, nutmeg, mace, sugar candy on a brandy base. Drink it straight or mix it with white crème de cacao or vodka.

Falernum is a syrup with a low alcoholic content made with almonds, limes, ginger and other spices. It is used more for flavoring than as a cordial.

Frangelico liqueur is imported from Italy. Its smooth hazelnut taste is best enjoyed straight or on the rocks.

Pistàshà, the pistachio nut liqueur. Try it with brandy, with vodka or in the following delicious combination:

Blend together: 3/4 oz. Pistàshà
1-1/4 oz. vodka
3/4 oz. cream of coconut
2 oz. pineapple juice
3/4 cup crushed ice
Garnish with fruit slice and serve in a brandy snifter.

Chocolate almond combines widely appreciated flavors. Try it with milk, cherry flavored brandy, with vodka, with brandy, with peppermint schnapps or over vanilla ice-cream.

A Taste of Orange, the Fruit of the Gods

THE GOLDEN APPLES

In Greek mythology there was an enchanted island called the Garden of the Hesperides. There grew the Golden Apples Juno had given to Jupiter on their wedding day. The three Hesperides, daughters of Atlas and Hespera, watched lovingly over the sacred fruit.

The fruits were so precious that the island was guarded by Ladon. He protected its many entrances but even a hundred-headed dragon like himself proved unable to fight off Hercules.

Hercules, who embarked on his twelve labors as a way to purify himself from the temporary insanity which had led him to kill his wife and children, landed on the island of the Hesperides to perform his next "labor." Of course, he completed his task successfully: he killed Ladon, stole the fruit and offered it to Athena. Athena, the virgin Goddess of Wisdom and Fertility, promptly returned the fruit to the Hesperides to avoid chaos and to reestablish the cosmic order, for she was also the Goddess of War, Peace and Mercy.

The oranges, divine fruits for the Greeks, symbolized for the Christians, fidelity in love and purity. Traditionally, brides wore wreaths of orange blossoms or carried them in their bouquets and the dried flowers became a precious memento and a reminder of love.

In medieval France, the orange tree was the tree of the kings. It appears in numerous tapestries, particularly in the Tapestry of the Thousand Flowers, the Lady of the Unicorn, and the oldest French tapestry in the Angers museum.

The most fabulous and historic orange tree was planted in Pamplona in Spain in 1421. It was then transported to Chantilly (where the famous cream comes from!), then to Fontainebleau. It belonged to the Grand Constable of France, the Duke of Bourbon. In 1523, the duke betrayed his king and fled to Spain. Francois I seized his estate and became the owner of the famous tree, the only one existing in France at the time. In 1663, the tree was moved to Versailles. Louis XIV ordered that an orangery be constructed to house the fabulous tree. After five centuries of glory, and by far outliving various monarchies, the tree finally died in Versailles about twenty years ago.

The history of oranges is a legend in itself. Sweet oranges, Confucious tells us, grew in the Chinese provinces of Chekiang and Kantung 500 years before Christ. However, they did not appear in Europe before the XVth century and the Europeans had to content themselves with bitter oranges brought to Spain by the Arabs in the IX century. Until the XVIIIth century, oranges were still a rare fruit, but cordials made with orange tree blossoms were in vogue. D'Alembert, one of the founder-editors of the XVIIIth century *Encyclopédie,* mentions in the article "Extract," that a liqueur made with orange flower water was prepared in Paris and sold under the name of "Divine Water."

Arab ships carried oranges from the Ganges Valley to the Red Sea ports. Then caravans transported them to Palestine before reaching the islands of the Mediterranean. This long and slow journey explains why oranges remained a luxury up until the advent of modern transportation.

CURACAO

It is the island of Curaçao that gave its exotic name to an orange liqueur born in the Caribbean. Originally it was a wine made with orange peels, then filtered and fermented. In the beginning of the XVIIth century, the Dutch, being experts in distillation, began to substitute alcohol for the wine and created a formula for a strong, mellow and aromatic liqueur. Curaçao soon enjoyed an extraordinary success, first among travelers, sailors and adventurers until it reached a much wider public.

In the XIXth century it was considered a proper drink for the ladies. When Emma Bovary entertained her future husband for the first time, she offered him a glass of Curaçao and even drank some of it herself.

As you choose the amber, blue, or white version of Curaçao, you bring into your home the gold of the sun, the deep blue of the sky, or the clear, clean waters of the Caribbean.

DRINKS

A Dream Island

1 oz. Blue curaçao
1 oz. light rum
1 oz. pineapple juice
Stir well, serve over crushed ice in transparent glasses.

Emerald Mist

1 oz. Blue curaçao
1½ oz. Irish Mist
Stir well and serve on the rocks.

There are not many "azure" drinks: these will transport you at once wherever you wish to be, like a flying carpet!

Curaçao and tonic
Curaçao Martinis

1½ oz. gin
1 oz. curaçao

1½ oz. vodka
1 oz. curaçao

1 oz. curaçao
1 oz. vodka
3 oz. dry vermouth

Combine in a mixing glass with ice cubes, stir gently to blend and strain into a chilled cocktail glass. Twist of orange peel instead of a lemon peel.

Curaçao Sour

2 oz. curaçao
juice of 1/2 a lemon
1/2 teasp of powdered sugar (optional)
Shake with cracked ice. Strain into cocktail glass.

ENTREES

SPARE RIBS

3 lbs. spare ribs cut in serving
  pieces
2 cloves minced garlic
3/4 cup curaçao
1/2 cup each ketchup or barbecue sauce and prepared
  mustard, preferably Dijon
  mustard.

Sprinkle ribs with salt and pepper to taste. Mix the remaining ingredients. Brush ribs with half the mixture. Put in a preheated 350° oven for one hour and a half. Keep brushing once in a while with pan drippings. When ribs are tender, brush with the remaining mixture and put under the grill for 10 minutes or until brown and crisp. Serves 4 to 6.

FLAMING STUFFED CHICKEN

1/2 cup each chopped celery
  and onion
1/2 cup butter (or margarine)
4 cups white bread cubes
1/2 cup coarsely chopped
  p e c a n s
1 teaspoon each salt and sage
1/2 teaspoon each pepper and
  thyme
1/2 cup Arrow orange curaçao
1 small navel orange, peeled,
  sectioned, and chopped
salt and pepper
5-6 lb. roasting chicken

In large skillet, cook celery and onion in butter until soft. Mix in bread cubes, pecans, salt, sage, pepper, thyme, ¼ cup curaçao, and orange. Sprinkle salt and pepper in chicken cavity. Stuff and truss chicken. Place chicken on rack in roasting pan. Bake in pre-heated 400° oven 2½ hours or until chicken is tender. Remove to heated serving platter. Warm remaining curaçao. Ignite and pour over chicken. When flame dies, immediately serve chicken and stuffing. Serves 6.

VEAL SCALLOPINI

4 thinly sliced veal cutlets
salt and pepper to taste
3 tbsps. butter or margarine
2 oz. beef consomme
2 oz. curaçao
2 tbsps. chopped parsley

Season cutlets with salt and pepper. Brown quickly on both sides in butter or margarine. Add beef consomme and curaçao. Simmer slowly 5 minutes. Put cutlets on heated serving platter. Pour sauce over them and garnish with parsley. Serves 4.

DESSERTS

FRUIT COMPOTE

Select your favorite canned or fresh fruits. Put in a large bowl. Add one tablespoon of curaçao per serving. Stir well. Chill at least 3 hours.

MELON BALLS

1 canteloupe
1 honeydew melon
4 oz. Arrow curaçao

Cut melons in half; using a bowl shape cutter scoop out melon balls. Marinate balls in shells with half the curaçao in each. Chill. Serve on toothpicks or mix and serve in cocktail glasses. Serves 4 to 6.

OMELETTE FLAMBE

Use your favorite omelette recipe but omit salt and add sugar to taste instead. When the omelette is ready put it on a serving dish. Pour one liqueur glass of curaçao over it and set aflame. Serve immediately.

AFTER DINNER DRINKS

Curaçao frappe
Curaçao on the rocks (your favorite color)
Curaçao straight
Curaçao & brandy

1 oz. curaçao
1 oz. brandy or cognac

Serve straight or on the rocks. Or add 1 oz. lemon juice shake with ice, strain and serve in cocktail glass rimmed with powdered sugar.

Ladies Luck

1 oz. Marie Brizard anisette
1 oz. Arrow curaçao

Shake with ice, strain in cocktail glass.

Crepes Flambees

Cafes and Cointreau to linger over...

COINTREAU LIQUEUR

The Caribbean was also a source of inspiration for one of the best known French liqueurs: Cointreau. Two Cointreau brothers founded a distillery in the historic town of Angers in the Loire Valley soon after the Revolution. The setting was perfect. The Anjou province is known as one of the gardens of France. They first manufactured Guignolet, a cherry liqueur made from the guigne, a local cherry and also fruit candies. Edward Cointreau, the son of the founder, loved to travel and felt the need to expand the family business. He went to the English and Dutch colonies in the Caribbean and in South America. There, he discovered small wild bitter oranges native to the islands and this is how Cointreau was born. At that time, the fruits could not have survived the voyage so he shipped the dried peels of those oranges to Angers. His father experimented with them, mixed them with other kinds of oranges, bitter and sweet, immersed them in high quality spirits with other secret ingredients, distilled them not once but twice and arrived at the formula still used today. He was the first to make such a very dry liqueur (according to the standards of the time) — three times drier in fact. So popular was this new drink, that imitations proliferated under the name of triple sec. He decided then, to name the liqueur he had invented after himself, and to this day it is called Cointreau.

The unique, crystal clear liqueur with a bite is still made today by the descendants of its inventor. Its formula is still secret. The firm has grown so since the 1860's that today it also offers a wide selection of fine liqueurs besides Cointreau, under the name of Regnier.

DRINKS

Cointreau and tonic on the rocks in a tall glass.

Side Car:

1 oz. Cointreau
1 oz. cognac
2 oz. fresh lemon juice
Shake well with ice, strain and serve in a chilled cocktail glass.

White Lady:

1 oz. Cointreau
1 oz. gin
1 oz. fresh lemon juice
Shake well with ice, strain in a stem glass.

Champagne Cocktail:

1 to 2 oz. of Cointreau
and chilled champagne to your taste.

Margarita:

1/2 oz. Cointreau
1 oz. tequila
1 oz. lemon juice
Shake with ice and strain into a chilled cocktail glass.

Between the sheets:

1 oz. Cointreau
1 oz. rum
1 oz. brandy
1/4 oz. fresh lemon juice
Shake with cracked ice and strain into a chilled cocktail glass.

ENTREES

SOLE AU GRATIN ON MUSHROOMS

8 fillets of sole
2½ lbs. mushrooms
4 tablespoons vinegar
2 tablespoons Cointreau
3/4 cup oil
1 tablespoon minced parsley
1 tablespoon grated onion
1 tablespoon minced chives
1 pinch thyme
1 teaspoon dried tarragon
1 onion, sliced
A few celery leaves
1 cup dry white wine
3 oz. French brandy
2 egg yolks
1/4 lb. Swiss cheese
Butter, flour, salt and pepper

Marinate finely chopped mushrooms in mixture of vinegar, Cointreau, oil, parsley, grated onion, chives, thyme and tarragon. Forty minutes before serving, simmer fillets of sole for 15 to 20 minutes in broth composed of the sliced onion, celery leaves, wine, brandy and enough water to cover. When cooked, set aside. Saute mushroom marinade in butter for 2 minutes. Drain and transfer to shallow baking dish. Place the fillets of sole on the mushrooms. Prepare a white sauce with flour and part of the fish stock. Add the Swiss cheese (broken up). Simmer until the cheese is melted and at the last minute, slowly add the lightly beaten egg yolks. Serves 8.

DUCKLING a L'ORANGE

1 duckling (2 to 3 lbs.)
6 oranges
1 cup glazed meat sauce
2 lumps sugar
3 tablespoons vinegar
1/2 cup Cointreau

Clean and dress duckling. Roast until brown. Deglaze the sauce from roasting pan. Add juice of 2 oranges and the peel of 2 oranges cut in small strips about the size of kitchen matchsticks, first poached for 3 minutes. In a small saucepan, dissolve sugar to caramel consistency. Add vinegar, glazed meat sauce and Cointreau Liqueur. Do not boil. Carve duckling and cover with the sauce. Slice remaining 2 oranges as garnish. Serves 4.

RIZZOTTO AU COINTREAU

1 cup rice
2 tablespoons butter
1 can clear beef bouillon
6 tablespoons tomato puree
2 tablespoons flour (for sauce)
3 oz. water
2 tablespoons Cointreau
Parmigiano cheese (optional)
Salt, pepper

Saute rice with butter in sauce pan for 3 to 4 minutes and until slightly brown. Mix constantly. Add a little bouillon and bring to a boil. While boiling, add more bouillon—a little at a time. Cover and cook 25 to 35 minutes, adding more bouillon, if necessary. While rice is cooking, prepare Light Brown Sauce: (Recipe can be found in any cook book.) Fold in puree of tomatoes and water. Salt and pepper to taste. Simmer for 15 to 20 minutes, then add Cointreau Liqueur. When rice is cooked, mix together with sauce. If grated cheese is used, sprinkle over entire surface before serving. Serves 6.

114

DESSERTS:

CREPES FLAMBEES

Crêpes
2 eggs
2 egg yolks
1 cup milk
1 tbsp. Cointreau
2 tbsps. butter or margarine
3/4 cup flour
1 tbsp. sugar
1/2 tsp. salt

Beat to combine eggs, egg yolks, milk, Cointreau, melted butter. Stir in dry ingredients until smooth. Heat 6 or 7-inch skillet; brush with butter. Pour in 2 tbsps. batter, tilting pan to spread. Brown both sides. Repeat with rest of batter. Makes about 16 crêpes.

Sauce
12 small sugar cubes
1 large orange
6 tbsps. butter
2 tbsps. sugar
2 Tbsps. sugar

Rub sugar cubes over skin of orange to absorb its oil. Squeeze orange and reserve juice. Melt 3 tbsps. butter in chafting dish pan. Drop in sugar cubes, press to crush. Add rest of butter, orange juice, ½ cup Cointreau, Heat, stirring until well mixed.
Dip each crêpe in sauce and fold in quarters. When all are folded, sprinkle with sugar. Add ¼ cup Cointreau and tilt pan toward flame to ignite. Serves 6 to 8.

Quick Desserts

1 cup Cointreau
1 pint each chocolate and
   strawberry ice-cream

Pour 2 tsps. Cointreau into each of 8 parfait glasses. Top each with scoop of chocolate ice cream, another 2 tsps. Cointreau, scoop of strawberry ice cream. Warm remaining Cointreau, ignite and pour flaming over each serving. Serves 8.

FRUITS MINCEUR

Around two scoops of fruit sherbet, arrange an assortment of fresh fruits (strawberries, orange, cantaloupe, plum and mango slices and grapes). Moisten with Cointreau and garnish with fresh mint.

FRUITS IN COINTREAU SYRUP

Boil 2 cups sugar and 1 cup water to 230°. Remove from heat and stir in 1 cup Cointreau. For *kumquats* cut a cross in the stem end, parboil. Drain, then boil in Cointreau syrup until tender. For *cranberries,* gash the stem ends and boil in Contreau syrup until tender. For *tangerines* or *oranges* cut the fruit into thin slices, arrange tightly in a jar and cover with hot syrup. For *melons* peel firm fruit, cut in thin slices. Arrange in glass jars and cover with hot syrup. Pack, seal and store in a cool place. If you choose a pretty glass jar, fruits in syrup make lovely presents to bring to your friends.

AFTER DINNER DRINKS

Cointreau mixes very well with coffee:

COINTREAU DEMI-TASSE

In a demi-tasse, combine espresso and 1 tbsp. Cointreau.
Serve with an orange twist.

CAFE DIABLE

In a chafing dish, heat 1 cup coffee, 3 cinnamon sticks, a dash of all spice and cardamom, and one small piece orange rind. Add 2 jiggers Cointreau and 1 jigger cognac. Set ablaze. Add 2 cups hot strong coffee and 2 tbsps. sugar. Serve in tall heat-proof glasses with cinnamon sticks and orange zest strips. Makes 3 glasses.

FRENCH COFFEE

In a heat proof glass mug, stir in 1 jigger Cointreau with 1 tsp sugar and 6 oz. strong coffee. Top with Cointreau flavored whipped cream and sprinkle with slivers of orange peel.

MOCHA COFFEE

In a heat-proof glass mug, combine 1 oz. semi-sweet chocolate, 1 jigger Cointreau and 6 oz. strong coffee. Top with Cointreau flavored whipped cream and sprinkle with instant coffee.

COINTREAU; straight or with one ice cube in a snifter.

1 oz. Cointreau
1 oz. cognac
Straight or with an ice cube.

MORE ABOUT
CITRUS FRUIT LIQUEURS

Aurum: An orange flavored, sweet, gold colored Italian liqueur. Used mostly as an after dinner drink.

Citroengenever: It is a Dutch lemon liqueur with a zest in gin or neutral spirit base. It is excellent in hot or iced tea.

Cumquat: This sweet citrus liqueur is made from minature Japanese oranges grown on the sunny shores of Corfu. It is used mostly as an after dinner drink.

Forbidden fruit: a sweet liqueur which used to be made with citrus fruits, especially grapefruits, and now is also made with other fruits such as apples.

Grand Marnier: a sweet liqueur from France. It is distilled with the peels of oranges and blended with brandies. It started as a family enterprise in the XIXth century and is still one today. It is mostly used as an after dinner drink.

Mandarine Napoléon: a sweet cordial made from small tangerine type oranges on a fine Napoléon base. It is used mostly as an after dinner drink.

Parfait amour, may it keep your love life running smoothly, is made of orange and lemon peels, roses, almonds, coriander and other spices.

Sciarada: A tangy combination of citrus essences. Sciarada is delicious straight or on the rocks, or in mixed drinks, like:

"Sciarada Boccie": Pour a generous amount of Sciarada on the rocks, float a dash of brandy on top.

118

A Taste of Fresh Fruit

Peter Heering

(the flavor of cherries)

It would be lovely to enjoy a glass of Peter Heering at the Tivoli gardens in Copenhagen, among lights, laughter and music, or while dreaming near the Little Mermaid statue or sitting on top of Hamlet's castle on a rainy day. Impossible? Then dream and enjoy it at home—it is a most rewarding experience.

The Danes have coped with their northern climate by being hospitable and cheerful hosts. Imitate them with this 150 year old liqueur. Peter Heering is a family business and its formula is a family secret. We do know that only special cherries grown in the South New Zealand area are used and that the liqueur ages in ancient oak casks in the celebrated Peter Heering cellars. This aging process gives to the liqueur its particular flavor, body and aroma. It is light, full-blooded and delicately sweet.

DRINKS

Dry Mermaid Martini

1 part Peter Heering
4 parts gin
Shake well with ice and serve with a twist of lemon.

Hamlet

1 part Peter Heering
1 part Aquavit
Serve ice-cold. It will make you glow on a dark rainy night.

Wild Redhead

2 parts Peter Heering
1 part fresh lemon or lime juice
Shake with ice and serve in chilled glass or on the rocks.

Sparkling Champagne

Peter Heering (iced)
Champagne "BRUT" (iced)
Pour Peter Heering into chilled champagne glasses. Fill with Champagne.

On a hot day enjoy Peter Heering with tonic water or ginger ale in a tall glass with ice cubes.

ENTREES

BONELESS BIRDS

12 slices round steak ½ in. thick
1/4 lb. pork fat cut into 12 strips
1/4 cup chopped parsley
Salt and pepper to taste
2 tbsps. butter
1/4 cup Peter Heering
Boiling water

Pound beef slices with a mallet. On each slice, place a strip of pork fat and some of the chopped parsley, plus salt and pepper to taste. Roll the beef slices and secure with tooth-picks. Brown in butter, turning often. Then add boiling water to cover the meat. Simmer for about an hour or until tender. Boil gravy for a few minutes, add Peter Heering, and thicken with flour and butter. Serves 6.

APPLE SOUP

2 lbs. medium size apples,
   peeled, cored and sliced
4 cups of water
Cinnamon stick
2 slices white bread, crumbed
   very fine
Juice of one lemon
6 tbsps. sugar
2 cups Peter Heering

In a saucepan, combine apples, cinnamon; bread crumbs and water. Boiled over moderate heat until apples are soft. Strain apples, add lemon juice sugar and Peter Heering. Reheat over low heat until hot. Serves 6.

RHUBARB SOUP

1 tsp. cornstarch
1/2 cup sugar
2 sticks cinnamon
1/2 tsp nutmeg
2 tsp lemon juice
2 cups Peter Heering
2 cups water
2 cups finely cut rhubarb

Combine cornstarch, sugar and water. Heat, stirring until boiling point is reached. Add cinnamon, nutmeg, lemon juice, Peter Heering and rhubarb. Simmer for 5-10 minutes or until rhubarb is tender. Serves 4.

DESSERTS

Quick Desserts

Scoops of cherry vanilla ice-cream topped with 1 oz. Peter Heering.

A wine glass of Peter Heering mixed into drained dark sweet cherries over vanilla ice-cream.

Mix fresh strawberries with slivered almonds, cover with Peter Heering and chill. Serve with whipped cream if desire.

Favorite Danish dessert: cheese (blue, camembert, brie) served with a glass of Peter Heering.

AFTER DINNER DRINKS

With coffee

Red Dane

1 part vodka
1 part Peter Heering
Pour over ice cubes

Singapore Sling

1 part Peter Heering
2 parts gin
1/2 part Bénédictine
2 dashes bitters
1/2 oz. juice of lime or lemon
Sugar to taste

Pour all the ingredients in a large glass with ice cubes, stir well and add club soda to taste.

Apricot Flavored Brandy

Apricot is the fruit of the "Prunus Armeniaca" or plum tree from Armenia because it used to be considered a native of the Caucasus or Armenia. Later studies tend to suggest that it came from China, where the fruit is an emblem of the fair sex, and the slanting eyes of Chinese beauties are often compared to the ovoid kernels.

The ancient Persians used apricots, along with lemons and pomegranates to make sweet and sour sauces which gave a tang to their strong, fat mutton. Persian sweet and sour dishes were closer to those of China and India than to the ones of Classical Rome where a mixture of honey and vinegar prevailed.

The mission fathers brought apricots and other fruits to Southern California at the beginning of the XVIIIth century. The fruit now grows on the Pacific coast, in central and southeastern Asia, and in parts of southern Europe. The small, wild apricots from southern France and northern Africa, sun-ripened and flavorful, are particularly suited to make this luscious liqueur.

DRINKS

On the rocks
with club soda

Apricot Sour

1½ oz. apricot flavored brandy
¾ oz. lemon juice or lime juice

Shake over cracked ice, strain into chilled cocktail glass

Apricot and Rum

1 oz. apricot flavored brandy
1½ oz. rum
Juice of half a lime
Superfine sugar
Club soda

Pour rum and apricot flavored brandy in a tall glass half filled with cracked ice. Add lime juice and sugar to taste. Stir and fill with club soda.

ENTREES

CHICKEN BREASTS

6 chicken breasts boned
3 tbsps clarified butter
2 lemons cut into this slices
½ lb seedless grapes
2 oz. apricot flavored brandy

Cut chicken breasts into bite size pieces. Saute in butter until done. Add lemon slices and grapes, season with salt and pepper, add brandy and cook for another five minutes. Serves 6.

STEAKS WITH A DIFFERENCE

4 thin individual steaks
5 tbsps butter or margarine
1 tbsp chopped shallot
1 tbsp chopped chives
1 tbsp Worcestershire sauce
3 oz. apricot flavored brandy

Cook steaks to taste in 1 tbsp of butter or margarine in a heavy frying pan. Remove from pan and keep warm. Add remaining butter or margarine and saute shallots and chives until soft. Add Worcestershire sauce and apricot flavored brandy, cook for two or three minutes and pour over steaks. Serve immediately. Serves 4.

ESCALOPES DE VEAU

1½ lbs. veal cutlet
  sliced thin and pounded
Salt, pepper, paprika to taste
4 tbsps. butter or margarine
1/4 cup beef bouillon
1/4 cup Régnier apricot flavored
  brandy
2 cups sliced fresh mushrooms

Season veal with salt, pepper and paprika. Melt 3 tbsps butter or margarine in heavy skillet, brown meat quickly on both sides. Add bouillon and apricot flavored brandy and simmer 5 minutes or until meat is tender. Meanwhile, melt 1 tbsp butter or margarine in a small pan and brown mushrooms slightly. Add mushrooms to meat. Serves 4.

DESSERTS

APRICOT ALASKA

4 slices of pound cake
4 scoops vanilla ice-cream
4 tbsps. apricot preserve
6 oz. apricot flavored brandy
Whipped cream

Take out four large cocktail glasses or champagne glasses. In each put 1 slice pound cake, 1 scoop vanilla ice-cream and 1 tbsp apricot preserve. Add 1½ oz. apricot flavored brandy. Top with whipped cream. Serves 4.

APRICOT MOUSSE

2 cups fresh apricots
1/2 cup sugar
1 tbsp unflavored gelatine
2 tbsp lemon juice
2 oz. apricot flavored brandy
2 cups whipped cream

Soften gelatin in a small amount of cold water. Simmer pureed apricots, sugar, lemon juice for a few minutes. Add softened gelatin, apricot flavored brandy, blend well and chill. When chilled add 2 cups whipped cream and mix well. Pour into 4 serving dishes and freeze. Serves 4.

AFTER DINNER DRINKS

On the rocks

Apricot Alexander

1½ oz. apricot flavored brandy
1/2 oz. white crème de cacao
1 oz. cream

Shake with ice and pour unstrained into on-the rocks glass.

Cranberry Liqueur

Cranberries are part of the American Indian folklore. They are the only berries found exclusively in North America. A giant mastodon was the beast of burden for all other animals, but he thought of himself as their king. One day he rebelled against this constant humiliation and caused a huge battle. The fighting ended with the intervention of the Great Spirit: he hurled lightning bolts at the combattants. The land was ravaged, and turned into a bog. Then the Great Spirit covered the devastated ground with green vines, which later blossomed and gave a bright red fruit: the cranberries. They became a symbol of peace for the Sachems of the Delawares.

Cranberries played an important part in the American Indian diet. They used the berries as a poultice against blood poisoning and as a dye for clothes and blankets. The Indians introduced the red fruit to the pilgrims. The newcomers thought its flowers resembled the head of a crane, so they called it crane-berry which was later shortened to cranberry. The pioneers moved westward and took cranberries with them to ward off scurvy, just as the New England sailors did in the days of clipper ships and whaling voyages. This is how cranberries were brought to Wisconsin, Washington state, Oregon and some parts of Canada.

Andrew Rider, founder of Rider College in Trenton, New Jersey, brought cranberries to the Continent. He took several cases with him on the ship. His great ambition was to make Queen Victoria fond of the new fruit. He succeeded and England became an excellent customer for the cranberries Rider was growing in his own bogs in New Jersey.

This is quite a remarkable fruit: the flowers are unusual, the fruit is glorious. The bogs at harvesting time, in autumn, are a magnificent sight; as beautiful as New England autumn leaves. In the winter they are flooded to protect the vines from extreme temperatures and then they become convenient skating rinks. The fruit makes a delicious cordial in all seasons.

Although cranberries are part of the American tradition during Thanksgiving and Christmas, and although they don't grow in France, it was the French House of Cointreau that started the trend of cranberry liqueur.

DRINKS:

Red Russian:
2 oz. Cranberria Liqueur
1 oz. vodka
A twist of lime
Stir and serve on the rocks. Splash of club soda: optional.

A refreshing drink:
2 oz. cranberry liqueur in tall glass with ice cubes, fill with club soda.

Champagne and Cranberry Liqueur

4 oz. Champagne (chilled)
1 oz. cranberry liqueur
Serve in chilled champagne glasses.

White wine and Cranberry Liqueur

4 oz. dry white wine
1 oz. cranberry liqueur
Serve on the rocks in chilled wine glasses.

Dry White vermouth and Cranberry Liqueur

4 oz. dry white vermouth
1 oz. cranberry liqueur
Serve on the rocks in chilled wine glasses.

Boggs Fog

1 oz. orange juice
1 oz. vodka
1 oz. Boggs cranberry liqueur
Combine, stir briskly and serve over ice.

ENTREES

ROAST TURKEY WITH CRANBERRY SAUCE

1/2 cup each chopped onion and
  chopped celery
1/2 cup butter (or margarine)
1/2 lb. sausage meat, cooked,
  crumbled and drained
1 pkg. (8 oz.) herb seasoned
  stuffing mix
1 can (8 oz.) whole cranberry
  sauce
1/2 cup chopped pecans
1/4 cup Boggs Cranberry
  Liqueur
1/2 cup water
1 tablespoon instant chicken
  broth
1 teaspoon sage
1/2 teaspoon each salt and basil
10-12 lb. turkey
Salt and pepper
Oil

In large skillet cook onion and celery in butter until soft. Mix in sausage. stuffing mix, cranberry sauce, pecans, Boggs, water, broth, sage, salt and basil. Sprinkle turkey cavity with salt and pepper. Fill with stuffing mixture. Truss. Brush skin with oil. Place on rack in roasting pan. Roast in pre-heated 325° oven 3½-4 hours or until tender. Serve with Cranberry sauce. Serves 8-10.

CRANBERRY SAUCE

1 can (8 oz.) whole cranberry
  sauce
1/4 cup orange juice
1/4 cup Boggs Cranberry
  Liqueur
2 tablespoons brown sugar

In small saucepan mix all ingredients. Bring to boil. Reduce heat. Simmer 15 minutes or until slightly thickened. Serve with roast turkey. Makes 1½ cups. Serves 8 to 10.

SWEET N' SOUR PORK CHOPS

6 center cut pork chops, 1"
  thick, trimmed
Salt and pepper to taste
1 medium onion, sliced
1 medium clove garlic, minced
1 small green pepper, diced
3/4 cup Boggs Cranberry
  Liqueur
1 can (8 oz.) pineapple chunks,
  undrained
Juice of 1 fresh lemon
1 tablespoon Japanese soy
  sauce
1 package (10 oz.) frozen
  Chinese pea pods
2 tablespoons sliced pimientos
2 tablespoons cornstarch
3 tablespoons water

In large skillet brown chops well on both sides. Sprinkle with salt and pepper. Add onion, garlic, Boggs, pineapple, lemon juice, green pepper, and soy sauce. Simmer 1 hour or until chops are tender. Combine cornstarch and water. Blend into pan liquid. Add pea pods and pimientos. Continue simmering 5 minutes or until pods are tender crisp. Serve on bed of rice. Serves 4-6.

CRANBERRY CANDIED YAMS

1/4 cup butter (or margarine)
2 tablespoons brown sugar
1/2 cup Boggs cranberry
  liqueur
1 teaspoon finely grated orange
  rind
1 can (24 oz.) yams, drained
  and sliced

In large skillet melt butter with brown sugar, Boggs and orange rind. Place potato slices in syrup. Simmer 3-4 minutes on each side or until well glazed. Serves 4-6.

ROSY-RED BEETS

1/2 cup Boggs cranberry
    liqueur
2 teaspoons cornstarch
1 can (16 oz.) sliced beets,
    drained
1 small onion, sliced and
    separated into rings
1/2 teaspoon salt
1/4 cup sour cream

In small saucepan mix Boggs and cornstarch. Cook over medium heat until clear and slightly thickened. Mix in beets, onion and salt. Heat thoroughly. Remove from heat and stir in sour cream. Serve immediately. Serves 4.

DESSERTS:

CRANBERRY-PEACH MELBA

1/4 cup sugar
1 teaspoon cornstarch
1 pkg. (10 oz.) frozen raspberries,
    pureed and strained
3/4 cup Boggs cranberry
    liqueur
1 can (29 oz.) cling peach halves,
    drained
1 qt. vanilla ice cream

In small saucepan, mix sugar and cornstarch. Mix in raspberries and Boggs. Simmer, stirring constantly, until sauce is slightly thickened. Chill. Top peach half with vanilla ice cream. Spoon sauce over all. Serves 6-8.

DESSERT FRUIT SOUP

2 cups Boggs cranberry liqueur
1/2 lb. pitted dried prunes
1/4 lb. dried apricots
1 cup seedless raisins
2 tablespoons quick-cooking
  tapioca
1/2 cup sugar
1 stick cinnamon
3 apples, diced
1 orange, thinly sliced
1 lemon, thinly sliced
4 cups water

Place all ingredients in 4 quart saucepan. Bring to a boil. Reduce heat. Simmer, covered, 30 minutes. Chill several hours or overnight. Serves 10-12.

FROSTY FRUIT COMPOTE

1 can (11 oz.) mandarin oranges,
  drained
1 can (20 oz.) pineapple chunks,
  drained
1/2 cup Boggs cranberry
  liqueur
Coconut

Mix oranges, pineapple and cranberry liqueur. Place in freezer 2 hours or until fruits begin to get icy. Spoon into individual dessert dishes and sprinkle with coconut. Serve immediately. Serves 4-6.

In season, use fresh fruits instead of canned fruits.

CRANBERRIA VACHERIN

3 tablespoons cornstarch
1/3 cup sugar
1/2 cup Cranberria Liqueur
1½ cups water
6 egg whites
1/2 tablespoon cream of tartar
2 cups sugar
1 qt. strawberries
1 qt. vanilla ice cream
2 cups sliced fresh or canned
  peaches

In sauce pan, mix corn starch with 1/3 cup sugar. Add Cranberria and water and stir over medium heat until sauce thickens and bubbles. Cover and chill. Beat egg whites with cream of tartar until stiff. Gradually beat in sugar, using 2 tablespoons at a time until mixture is stiff and glossy. Line cookie sheet with foil and mark an eight inch diameter circle lightly on foil. Spread half of meringue on foil to make a layer 8 inches in diameter about ½ inch thick. Place remaining meringue in pastry bag with a star tip and pipe meringue around edge of mound, shaping an edge. Bake in pre-heated oven at 275° for one hour or until dry and crisp. Turn oven off and let cool in oven. Hull strawberries and slice half the berries. Shape ice cream into scoops and place in freezer. When ready to serve, place meringue on serving platter and fill with sliced strawberries, ice cream balls and peach slices.

Place whole strawberries around base of meringue. Spoon sauce over fruit and ice cream. Serve remaining sauce over each serving. Serves 8 to 10.

AFTER DINNER DRINKS

Cranberry liqueur straight or on the rocks

Cranberry liqueur Frappé with a twist of lime

Blackberry Flavored Brandy

Blackberries are the fruit of the wild bramblebush. They were so common that no legend, superstition or special virtues seemed to surround them. And, yet one can still say today with Shakespeare: "If reasons were as plentiful as blackberries..." (Henry IV, Part I, Act II, Scene IV, Line 269) They are pretty to look at, taste very good and some say the blacker the berries, the sweeter the juice! The American Indians already knew that: the berries were an intrinsic part of their diet. In time, of course, they taught the settlers new ways to use and serve them.

They may not be romantic or mysterious but they are the main ingredient of a delicious and very popular liqueur: the blackberry flavored brandy.

DRINKS

Blackberry beauty cocktail

4 parts blackberry flavored brandy
1 part fresh lime juice

Strain over ice into a chilled cocktail glass.

Blackberry flavored brandy and club soda:

Serve on the rocks with a wedge of lime.

Blackberry vermouth:

1 oz. blackberry flavored brandy
2 oz. dry vermouth

Shake with ice cubes and pour into cocktail glass, or in a tall glass if you want to add soda water.

BLACKBERRY HAMBURGERS

1 lb. lean ground beef (top
  round or sirloin)
1/4 cup soft bread crumbs
  (optional)
Salt and pepper to taste
blackberry flavored brandy
Butter or margarine, or half
  butter or margarine and oil

In a mixing bowl, combine beef,
bread crumbs, salt, pepper. Shape into
4 patties. Brown in butter or margarine
or in half butter and margarine and
oil. Cook hamburgers to taste. Remove
hamburgers from the pan, keep warm.
To pan juices, add 2 tbsps. of butter and
¼ cup blackberry flavored brandy;
blend thoroughly and pour over
hamburgers.

You can do the same thing with thin
steaks. In the last step, add chopped
parsley and a dash of Worcestershire
sauce. Serves 4.

SPICY SAUCE FOR BOILED BEEF OR LEFT-OVER POT-ROAST

1/4 cup wine vinegar
1 tbsp. sugar
1 cup beef broth (home-made,
  canned or prepared with one
  beef bouillon-cube)
1 teaspoon cornstarch
1/4 cup blackberry flavored
  brandy
1/8 teaspoon ground cinnamon
1/8 teaspoon ground cloves
1/3 cup assorted dried mixed
  fruits cut into small pieces.
5 tbsps. raisins
1 tbsp. grated orange rind
2 teaspoons fresh lemon juice.

Put sugar and vinegar in a saucepan.
Bring to a boil and cook 5 minutes
stirring constantly. Add broth and stir
until well blended. Dissolve cornstarch
in blackberry brandy and add to
the saucepan. Cook and stir until
clear. Add remaining ingredients
and simmer for a few minutes.

DESSERTS

Blackberry flavored brandy is excellent over melon, peaches, pears and grapefruit.

BLACKBERRY YOGURT

8 oz. fresh or frozen blackberries
1 pint yogurt
2 oz. blackberry flavored brandy

Combine all the ingredients in blender. Blend until smooth. Garnish with berries. Serves 4.

CUBAN BANANAS

3 tbsps. butter
2 tbsps. brown sugar
1/4 tsp. cinnamon
3 oz. blackberry flavored brandy
6 bananas (not too ripe) cut
   lengthwise

Melt butter in a chafing dish or a skillet. Add sugar, cinnamon and blackberry flavored brandy. Stir in bananas. Cook briefly on each side so that bananas remain firm. Baste with pan syrup. Serve immediately. Serves 6 to 8.

AFTER DINNER DRINKS

Straight or on the rocks.

   2 oz. blackberry flavored brandy
   1 oz. vodka
Stir well and serve on the rocks.

   2 oz. blackberry flavored brandy
   1 oz. light rum
Stir well and serve on the rocks.

Crème De Cassis

The virtues of blackcurrants have been known for a long time. In the Middle Ages, black currants were believed to cure colds and snake-bites. At the beginning of the XVIIIth century, Bailly de Montaran, a Sorbonne scholar, wrote a little volume singing the praises of cassis. It was so successful that it was reprinted in 1750 in several French towns. Bailly de Montaran seemed to consider cassis a ubiquitous remedy: good for smallpox, gout, migraine, cuts, swelling of the stomach, melancholy, and so on. In many households, a medicinal potion based on blackcurrants was made and used as the "cure it all" remedy. The growing reputation of cassis inspired Monsieur Lagoutte, the only Dijon liqueur maker of the time, to perfect the local formula. The blackcurrant liqueur of Dijon, the modern crème de cassis, became very popular. As a result, the cultivation of blackcurrants grew rapidly in Burgundy.

The Burgundy region of France has at least two very good reasons to account for its reputation: the quality of its wines and the excellence of its blackcurrants. Dijon, Burgundy's capital, is where the best cassis is grown.

Nowadays, the drink that combines the qualities of wine and crème de cassis has acquired a world wide reputation: it is called a Kir. It was invented during World War II by Canon Felix Kir, a Dijon-born priest and hero of the French Resistance. It is said that he invented that particular drink because at the time there was a surplus of Aligoté, a white wine from the region.

DRINKS

Kir:

3 oz. dry Burgundy white wine
1 oz. crème de cassis (or less if you want a drier drink)
Stir with ice, strain into wine glass.

You can of course choose a dry white wine other than a Burgundy, but then it will not be called a Kir but a Vin Blanc Cassis. A good suggestion is to use in your Kir the same wine you will be drinking at dinner.

Vermouth Cassis:

2 oz. dry vermouth
1 oz. crème de cassis

Shake over ice, strain into cocktail glass. If you feel like a long drink, strain into a tall glass and add club soda.

Gin Cassis:

1½ oz. gin
1/2 oz. crème de cassis
Shake over ice, strain into cocktail glass.

Vodka Cassis:

1½ oz. vodka
1/2 oz. crème de cassis
Shake over ice, strain into cocktail glass.

ENTREES

ROCK CORNISH HENS CASSIS

4 Rock Cornish hens (about 1 lb. each)
Salt, pepper to taste
4 tablespoons butter
1/2 cup Régnier crème de cassis
1 teaspoon ground ginger

Season hens with salt and pepper, rub with butter, arrange on a rack in a baking pan. Roast in hot oven (425°) 15 minutes. Blend crème de cassis with ginger, brush on hens. Lower heat to 325°, roast 15 minutes longer, or until the flesh of the drumstick feels soft to pressure and the legs move easily. Pour remaining glaze over the birds in serving platters. Serves 4.

CHERRY SOUP CASSIS

2 cans (1 lb. each) waterpacked sour red cherries
4 teaspoons cornstarch
1 cup Régnier crème de cassis
4 tablespoons sugar
1/2 teaspoon salt
1/2 teaspoon cinnamon
Rind of 1 orange

Drain cherries, reserving 1 cup of the juice. Puree fruit, juice and remaining ingredients in a blender. Or force cherries through a sieve and grate the orange rind finely; combine. Stir over moderate heat until soup boils. Serve hot or cold, with sour cream. Serves 6.

DESSERTS

Crème de Cassis over lime sherbet

Crème de Cassis over vanilla ice-cream

Cassis Rainbow in parfait glasses, put layers of different flavored and colored ice-cream or sherbet. Between each of the layers, pour a little crème de cassis. Put some on top too, and finish with whipped cream.

Make a salad of your favorite fresh fruits and pour crème de cassis over them. Chill.

PEACH CASSIS

6 fresh peach halves, peeled
2 oz. crème de cassis
2 oz. peach flavored cordial
6 oz. raspberry or strawberry
  puree
1 qt. vanilla ice-cream

First prepare a simple syrup: in saucepan, put 1 cup water, 1½ cup sugar, a vanilla bean, cook for 5 minutes. Poach peaches for 10 minutes in syrup. Remove peaches. Pour peach cordial over them. Chill thoroughly. Mix crème de cassis with raspberry or strawberry puree and chill also. Put peach halves on vanilla ice-cream, top with cassis/raspberry or strawberry mixture. You can also serve the peaches without ice-cream. Serves 6.

AFTER DINNER DRINKS

On the rocks.

Cassis Sour:

1 ½ oz. crème de cassis
Juice of half a lemon or lime
Shake in cracked ice, strain into snifter

Rum Cassis:

1 ½ oz. light rum
1/2 oz. crème de cassis
Juice of ½ lime
Stir in a glass full of cracked ice, add a splash of club soda.

MORE ABOUT FRUITS

One of the best ways to enjoy fruits all year around, even out of season, is to enjoy a fruit liqueur. There was a time when cordials were made only with a few varieties of fruits, but now the possibilities are infinite.

BANANAS

Banana nectar:
made in Hawaii and other islands with bananas, spices and sugar on a rectified spirit base. Tastes just like fresh bananas.

Crème de banana:
a cordial with the pleasant fragrance of fresh bananas.

CHERRIES

Cherry Bestle:
a liqueur made from a special kind of Danish cherries and secret spices.

Cherry flavored brandy:
depending on the house producing it, this is made from bitter sweet cherries, with or without their crushed stones, on a base of brandy or neutral spirit.

Maraschino:
This cordial keeps the pleasant taste of the bitter-sweet marasca cherries which come from the dalmatian part of Yugoslavia.

COCONUTS

Mary Brizard Coconut Liqueur:
A nice flavor from the tropics.

MANGOS

Mango liqueur:
a cordial made from the mango fruit in Hawaii.

MELONS

Suntory Midori liqueur:
flavored with Japanese honeydew melon; it combines a rich fragrance and a refreshing mysterious taste.

PAPAYAS

Papaya liqueur:
is made in Hawaii with papaya juice, rectified spirit, spices and sugar syrup. It is enjoyable straight or as a frappe.

PASSION FRUITS

Passion fruit cordial:
it is made with the fruit of the passion tree, sugar, spices on a rectified spirit base. It is very pleasant in a cocktail with rum, grenadine, lime or lemon juice over cracked ice.

PEACHES

Peach flavored brandy:
recaptures the taste of fresh peaches and can be used in the same drink and dishes as apricot brandy.

PINEAPPLES

Crème d'ananas:
a pineapple flavored cordial, very good in rum cocktails.

PEARS

Marie Brizard Pear William liqueur:
the subtle and rich fragrance of pears.

If you are fond of the delicate flavor of ripe pears, try mixing 2 oz. of Pear William and 1 oz. cognac, or on a cold day comfort yourself with Hot Pear William: pour 2 oz. of Pear Williams into 8 oz. of hot apple juice. Add lemon wedges studded with cloves and cinnamon sticks.

PRUNELLES (WILD PLUMS)

Liqueur de prunelle:
made from the meat of the plum pit, figs, sugar, vanilla bean and neutral spirit.

Prunelle:
a cordial made from a small wild plum which grows in Burgundy (France). The base is brandy, sweetened with sugar.

Sloe Gin:
It is the most popular American wild plum cordial. It is called sloe gin but it is not a gin. It is made from sloe berries growing on blackthorn bushes. It owes its name to the fact that at the beginning of the century, the base was gin especially in England, but now it is neutral spirit.

Sloe gin is a pleasant experience on the rocks, with soda water and a dash of sugar and lemon juice, or with orange and apple juices.

QUINCES

Quince cordial:

a sweet and fragrant mixture of cinammon, coriander, ginger and nutmeg steeped in brandy, then a fairly large quantity of fresh quince juice is add with sugar.

RASPBERRIES

Raspberry liqueur:

a deep red, sweet liqueur which recaptures the flavor of fresh raspberries

Wild raspberry liqueur:

(Fraises des bois in French) brings back the subtle fragrance of fresh wild raspberries.

Cloudberries are a variety of wild raspberries, they are yellowish red and the Finns make a nice cordial with them.

STRAWBERRIES

Several houses make strawberry flavored cordials. Their color is beautiful and their taste is a constant reminder of the fresh flavor of strawberries.

Banana, cherry, tropical fruits, raspberry, strawberry cordials are deliciou on the rocks, with club soda, or mixed with rum with a dash of lime juice.

A Taste of Anise

ANISE AND ABSINTHE

The anise plant came from the Near East but it spread quickly to Europe and Asia. Its popularity began in ancient times and it has not diminished to this day. Assyrians used the anise plant as a medicine; Romans used it as a digestive in their banquets. In the Middle Ages it was a charm against bad dreams and the "evil eye." Nowadays some people drink anise seed tea as a reliever of fever, coughing fits and asthma. Others consider anisette, the liqueur made from the anise seeds, as one of the best remedies against motion sickness.

Another variety of anise seed is the star anise. It comes from a magnolia type tree found in Southern China. It yields an aroma and a flavor almost identical to that of the seed of the anise plant, although some experts claim that the star anise is more pungent. Shaped like a star, dried star anise is beautiful, and in the Orient it is often regarded as a good luck charm.

Licorice root and fennel seeds have a flavor similar to that of anise and are often used in the making of anisette liqueurs. Many companies produce their own type of anisette but Mary Brizzard is one of the oldest and most famous French anisettes. Just ask for a Marie Brizzard in a French cafe and they'll know you want an anisette.

It's impossible to mention anisette without talking about absinthe, a liqueur made of many aromatic herbs whose taste was drier and bitter but still similar to anise. Its name however comes from a very particular herb, Absinthia Artesimium, commonly called wormwood. It was prescribed as a remedy against fever to the French troops during the conquest of Algeria in 1830-37. Its popularity grew to the point that the aperitif hour in France began to be called the green hour. It was also very popular in England in Edwardian days, but some women, finding it too dry, used to sweeten the liqueur by pouring it over a sugar cube placed on the special "absinthe spoon."

Such a popular drink had to have its place in literature and it does. Absinthe appears frequently in accounts of French literary and artistic circles. Zola immortalized the horrible effects of absinthe poisoning in *L'Assomoir*. Renoir painted a beautiful actress in *The End of Lunch*, and Degas chose the same one as a model. She is shown ravaged by the green drink in his famous painting *Le Cafe*, which is better known as *l'Absinthe*, and is suffused with a malevolent green light. The destructive side effects of absinthe—the most famous is the fit of madness which compelled Van Gogh to cut his ear—caused many countries to ban it in its original form at the beginning of the XXth century. Today anisette is made of anise seeds, licorice, fennel, aromatic herbs, but not wormwood.

Carrot Puree Marie Brizard

MARIE BRIZARD ANISETTE

The reign of Louis XVth can be remembered for its graceful furniture, refinement, luxurious clothes for men and women, flashing jewels, exquisite snuff boxes, powdered wigs bending over gaming tables piled with gold, the music of young Mozart, Mme. de Pompadour and Mme. du Barry, the King's glamourous favorites, but also its poverty, famines, epidemics and pestilence. The court lived in elegance, continuous entertainment and intrigue, while the poor suffered. But those troubled times also saw the birth of an extraordinary liqueur.

Marie Brizard was the daughter of a carpenter. During an epidemic which was raging through France, she nursed a West Indian back to health. To show his gratitude, he gave her the recipe of an anise elixir of his own invention and assured her it could cure many ills. We would like to think that he did not try it on himself because he fell in love with Marie Brizard and wanted her to take care of him. The charitable young woman tried this new medicine with a great deal of success. The sick she helped not only got better but kept asking for it and drinking it when they had recovered. The demand for this elixir grew so rapidly that she had to hire first her nephew and later a whole staff to help her . In 1755, the firm of Marie Brizard and Roger was founded and to this day produces the Marie Brizard Anisette and a range of ever increasing colorful and fragrant liqueurs.

DRINKS

Misty Marie:
Pour 3 ounces Marie Brizard anisette over ice cubes into old-fashioned glasses.
Ice, afloat in your Misty Marie, imparts a smoky mystique.
Serves 2.

Licorice Stick:
Combine 2 ounces Marie Brizard anisette and 6 ounces Marie Brizard brown cacao; pour over ice cubes. Add licorice stick stirrers. Serves 2.

Anisette Fizz:
Combine 4 ounces Marie Brizard anisette and 8 ounces club soda; pour into glasses over cracked ice.
Garnish with cinnamon sticks and lemon twists. Serves 2.

ENTREES

ICED POTAGE SENEGALESE

1 medium onion, thinly sliced
1 tablespoon butter or
  margarine
1/4 cup Marie Brizard anisette
2 teaspoons curry powder
1/4 teaspoon salt
white pepper
cayenne
4 cups chicken bouillon
3/4 cup dry white wine
3/4 cup unsweetened
  applesauce
1 cup finely diced cooked
  chicken
1 cup light cream

In medium saucepan, saute onion in butter until soft but not browned. Add anisette, curry powder, salt, a dash each of pepper and cayenne; cook over low heat, stirring constantly, 3 minutes. Add bouillon, wine and applesauce; bring to a boil. Cook over low heat, stirring frequently, 15 minutes. Cool slightly; puree in electric blender with chicken until smooth. Chill thoroughly. Before serving, stir in cream. If desired, garnish with a dollop of whipped cream and fresh dill. Serves 6.

SPICY BEEF ANISETTE

1 lb. bottom round steak,
  cut 1-inch thick
2 tablespoons butter or
  margarine
1/4 cup Marie Brizard anisette
1 medium onion, minced
1/4 teaspoon instant minced
  garlic
1 tablespoon flour
1 cup beef bouillon
1/4 cup raisins
1/4 teaspoon ginger
1/4 teaspoon salt
pepper (to taste)
1 large zucchini, cubed
2 tablespoons lemon juice

Cut steak into 1-inch cubes. Heat butter in medium saucepan; add meat and brown well on all sides. Heat anisette; pour over meat and ignite with a lighted match. When flame goes out, remove meat. Add onion and minced garlic to saucepan; cook, stirring constantly, until onion is tender. Mix in flour; cook, stirring constantly, until flour is lightly browned. Add bouillon, raisins, ginger, salt and a dash of pepper; bring to a boil, stirring constantly. Return meat to pan; simmer, covered, 1 hour. Add zucchini, cook 10 minutes. Remove from heat; stir in lemon juice. Serves 2.

LOBSTER IN CUCUMBER BOATS

1/2 cup Marie Brizard anisette
6 tablespoons lime juice
1/2 teaspoon salt
1 1/2 lbs. cooked lobster meat,
    diced
6 small cucumbers
1 cup mayonnaise
1/2 cup thinly sliced celery

Combine 6 tablespoons anisette, 4 tablespoons lime juice and salt. Put lobster meat in shallow dish; pour anisette mixture over lobster and toss gently to coat all surfaces. Cover and refrigerate at least 6 hours. Halve cucumbers lengthwise and hollow out centers to make "boats"; refrigerate until serving time. When ready to assemble salad, pour off marinade from lobster and stir into mayonnaise together with the remaining 2 table-spoons each of anisette and lime juice. Toss together lobster, celery and 2 tablespoons dressing. Spoon lobster salad into cucumber boats. Serve with remaining dressing. Serves 6.

CARROT PUREE MARIE BRIZARD

2 lbs. fresh carrots, peeled and
    quartered
salt and pepper (to taste)
boiling water
1/4 cup Marie Brizard anisette
1/4 cup heavy cream
1/4 cup butter or margarine
1/4 teaspoon bouquet garni

Cover and cook carrots in lightly salted boiling water until tender; drain. Thoroughly mash carrots with anisette, cream, butter, bouquet garni and a dash of pepper. Spoon into buttered 1 1/2 quart casserole. Bake in 400° oven 15 minutes or until hot. Serves 6.

149

FRUIT COMPOTE ANISETTE

2 cups water
1 cup sugar
1/3 cup Marie Brizard Anisette
2 tablespoons lemon juice
8 cups fresh cut fruit, such as: apples,
blueberries, grapefruit, grapes, melon
balls, oranges, pears, pineapple,
raspberries and strawberries

Combine water and sugar in medium
saucepan: bring to a boil, stirring
constantly. Simmer 3 minutes. Remove
from heat; stir in anisette and lemon
juice. Cool to room temperature. Pour
over fruit; mix gently, taking care not to
break the fruit. Chill at least 4 hours
before serving. Serves 10.

MOUSSE AU CHOCOLAT WITH FRENCH CREAM

2 packages (6 ounces each)
  semi-sweet chocolate pieces
1/2 cup Marie Brizard anisette
6 eggs, separated
1/4 teaspoon cream of tartar
1/2 cup superfine sugar
french cream
chopped pistachio nuts

In top of double boiler, melt chocolate
over hot (not boiling) water until just
melted; mix in *anisette* until smooth.
Remove from heat. Beat in egg yolks,
one at a time, beating well after each
addition. Cool to room temperature. In
large bowl, beat egg whites with
cream of tartar until soft peaks form.
Gradually beat in sugar; continue beating until stiff peaks form. Gently fold
chocolate mixture into egg whites.
Spoon into 10 individual dishes. Chill
thoroughly. Before serving, top with
French Cream and pistachio nuts.
Serves 10.
To make French Cream: Whip ½
cup heavy cream until stiff; fold in ½
cup sour cream, 1 tablespoon anisette
and 1 teaspoon sugar. Refrigerate until
serving time.

COFFEE ANISETTE CAKE

2¼ cups sifted cake flour
1½ cups sugar
3 teaspoons baking powder
1 teaspoon salt
1/2 cup salad oil
4 egg yolks
1/2 cup strong black coffee
1/4 cup Marie Brizard anisette
1/2 teaspoon grated lemon peel
8 egg whites
1/2 teaspoon cream of tartar

Sift together flour, sugar, baking powder and salt into mixing bowl; make a well in center. In this order, add oil, egg yolks, coffee, anisette and lemon peel. Beat until satiny. In a large bowl, combine egg whites and cream of tartar; beat until very stiff peaks form. Pour egg yolk batter in thin stream over whites; gently fold together. Turn into 2 ungreased, waxed paper-lined 9-inch layer cake pans. Bake in 350⁰ oven 40 minutes. Cool in pans.

Cream Filling and Frosting
3 cups heavy cream
2 teaspoons instant powdered
  coffee
2 tablespoons sugar
1/3 cup Marie Brizard anisette

Combine cream, coffee and sugar; whip until stiff. Fold in anisette.

To assemble cake: Cut each cake into 2 layers. Spread cream on 3 layers; stack together. Top with fourth layer. Frost with remaining cream. Decorate as desired. Serves 10.

AFTER DINNER DRINKS
Espresso and Anisette

Pour 5 ounces of hot espresso coffee into demitasse cups.
Add 1 ounce Marie Brizard anisette
Garnish with lemon twists. Serves 2.

Cocoa Brizard

Combine 3 ounces Marie Brizard anisette and
12 ounces hot cocoa; pour into mugs. Garnish with marshmallows.
Serves 2.

Deep Gold

*Combine 4 ounces Marie Brizard anisette and
2 ounces Marie Brizard blackberry flavored brandy
in cordial glasses. Serves 2.*

Snowbird

*Combine 2 ounces Marie Brizard anisette,
4 ounces lemon sherbet and 1 cup ice cubes in blender.
Blend 1 minute or until ice is crushed; pour.
Drinks may be placed in freezer for 30 minutes.*

SAMBUCA ROMANA

The essential ingredient of Sambuca is beautiful and sweet-smelling: it is the white flowers of the elderbush which grows all through Europe, particularly on Italian hillsides and along English lanes. It blooms in all its glory in late June or early July.

The name Sambuca comes from the Latin name of the elderbush, "Sambucus", which also gave its name to a very old musical instrument made from the hollow branches of the elderbush.

Since ancient times, the elderbush has been surrounded with countless stories about its extraordinary properties: it was planted near homes to repel evil spirits and witches. In 1655, a book entitled, *The Anatomy of the Elder*, was written to praise its medicinal virtues as a remedy against nasal congestion, croup hoarseness, colds and bronchitis. It was also said to bring down fever, and that is not all. The leaves, when bruised, give out a strong smell and were used before the advent of D.D.T. as insecticides to protect fruit, trees and vegetables.

Our grandmothers fought wrinkles and freckles with elderflower water; a soft cloth soaked in elderflower water and applied on the forehead was the remedy against headaches. They also made elderberry wine to sip on special occasions.

DRINKS

Romana Sour:

1 ½ oz. Sambuca Romana
1 oz. lemon juice
Club soda
Cherry, orange juice
Shake Sambuca Romana and lemon juice with ice. Strain over ice into Old Fashioned or Sour glass. Add splash of soda and fruit.

Pace Setter:

1 ½ oz. Sambuca Romana
Pinch of salt
Grapefruit juice, chilled
Lime slice
Pour Sambuca Romana over ice in 10 oz. glass. Add salt and grapefruit juice. Stir. Garnish with lime slice.

White Russian:

1 ½ oz. vodka
1/2 oz. Sambuca Romana
Pour over ice cubes in small Old Fashioned glass. Stir well. Twist orange peel over glass, drop in.

Sunny Sam:

1 oz. vodka
1/2 oz. Sambuca Romana
Orange juice, chilled
Lemon slice
Pour vodka and Sambuca Romana over ice in 8 oz. glass.
Add orange juice to fill. Garnish with lemon slice.

White Cloud:

1 oz. Sambuca Romana
Club soda, chilled
Pour Sambuca Romana over ice in a tall glass.
Add soda to fill.

Cool Banana:

1/4 oz. Sambuca Romana
1/4 oz. light rum
1 oz. lime juice
1/2 ripe banana
1 tsp. honey
1/4 cup crushed ice
Whirl in blender until smooth.
Pour into chilled cocktail glass.

Marion's Mark:

Place in container of electric blender:
Small scoop of shaved ice
1/4 oz. honey
1/2 oz. peach brandy
1/2 oz. Sambuca Romana
Juice of 1 lime
3 chunks of fresh pineapple
Mint leaves
Blend until frothy. Serve in large champagne glasses.
Decorate with sprig of mint leaf, fruit and speckle with
powdered sugar.

Blue Cloud:

2 oz. Sambuca Romana
1 oz. blue curaçao
Club soda
Fill large snifter with crushed ice. Pour over blue curaçao and Sambuca
Romana. Fill with club soda. Garnish with cherry, lemon and
orange slices. Serve with short straws.

Foreign Affair:

1 oz. brandy
1 oz. Sambuca Romana
Stir with ice and strain into cocktail glass.
Twist lemon peel over glass, drop in.

Roman Martini:

1 part Sambuca Romana
5 parts gin
Twist of lemon if desired.

Reunion (for 2):

1 oz. Sambuca Romana
1 oz. vodka

156

1 oz. strawberry liqueur
12 fresh, ripe strawberries (medium size), washed and hulled
6 oz. orange juice
2/3 cup crushed ice

Chill 2 large wine glasses.
Put all ingredients in blender and buzz until almost smooth.
Divide between 2 glasses.
Garnish with sprig of mint or fruit if desired.

ENTREES

SHRIMP CAPRI

1/4 cup Sambuca Romana
1/3 cup olive oil
2 tbsps. lemon juice
2 scallions, sliced
2 parsley sprigs
1 tsp. Worcestershire Sauce
1/2 tsp. tarragon
Salt, pepper — to taste
1/2 lb. cooked shrimp, shelled
1 large avocado, peeled and
  cubed

Buzz all ingredients except shrimp and avocado, in blender until smooth. Toss with shrimp and avocado. Chill. Serves 4.

POLLO VENETTO

2-3 tbsps. Sambuca Romana
2 tbsps. melted butter
Small lemon, grated rind and
  juice
1 garlic clove, crushed
1/4 tsp. thyme
Salt, pepper — to taste
2 whole chicken breasts, split

Combine all but chicken; spread mixture on both sides of chicken pieces. Place in pan, skin side up. Bake in preheated 350° oven about 1 hour, until tender and browned, basting with seasoning mixture and pan juices. Serves 4.

BAKED HAM ROMANA

1 canned, cooked boned ham,
  6-8 lbs.
1 unpeeled orange, thinly sliced
1/4 cup Sambuca Romana
1/2 cup brown sugar, packed
1 tbsp. vinegar
1 tbsp. mustard
2 tsps. Worcestershire sauce

Heat ham in oven according to package directions. Arrange orange slices on top of ham. Combine remaining ingredients, spoon over ham and oranges. Bake ½ hour or until glazed, basting with seasoning mixture.
Serves 12.

DESSERTS

If you are in a hurry, try the following dessert:
Substitute ¼ cup Sambuca Romana for ¼ cup water when preparing your favorite jello.

A special sauce for canned fruits;
     2 parts heavy cream
     1 part each Sambuca et fruit syrup from the can.

If you are in a more leisurely mood:

PEACH JUBILEE

2 tbsps. butter
1 large can cling peach
  halves, drained
3 tbsps. brown sugar
1/4 cup Sambuca Romana
Peach Ice cream

Melt butter in chafing dish. Add drained peaches, brown sugar. Heat thoroughly, turning once. Add Sambuca Romana, ignite. When flames burn out cover with ice cream.
Serves 6.

BISCOTTINI

24 ladyfingers
1/4 cup Sambuca Romana
1/2 cup softened butter
1/2 cup finely chopped almonds

Split ladyfingers. Thoroughly combine remaining ingredients. Spread mixture on flat side of each ladyfinger half. Place on cookie sheet. Toast in pre-heated 350° oven 6-8 minutes, until lightly brown. Cool. Store in covered container.

Sambuca Romana is delicious over chocolate or vanilla ice-cream.

AFTER DINNER DRINKS

Sambuca with Moscas:

Choose a tall, slender glass, pour Sambuca into it and float 3 or 5 coffee beans on top (please not 2 or 6)

Roman Kilt:

1 oz. scotch
1/2 oz. Sambuca Romana
Pour over crushed ice in small Old Fashioned glass.
Twist lemon peel over glass, drop in. Serve with small straw.

Roman Stinger:

1/2 oz. Sambuca Romana
1/2 oz. crème de menthe
1 oz. cognac
Shake with ice. Strain into cocktail glass.

White Velvet:

1½ oz. Sambuca Romana
1 egg white
1 tsp. lemon juice
1/3 cup crushed ice
Whirl in blender or shake very well.
Strain into large, chilled cocktail glass.

Roman Snowball:

Fill wine glass with shaved ice and mound top.
Add 1 oz. Sambuca Romana. Drink turns milky, like snowball.
Serve with short straws. Garnish.

Romana Caffe:

Add ½ oz. Sambuca Romana to a cup of hot black expresso
or regular coffee. Stir.

Crema Caffe:

1 oz. Sambuca Romana
1 oz. coffee liqueur
1 oz. cream
Shake with ice. Strain into cocktail glass.

Ermine Tail:

1 oz. Sambuca Romana
1/2 oz. cream
Instant espresso coffee powder
Pour Sambuca Romana in liqueur glass. Add cream, pouring over
back of spoon so it floats. Dust with espresso powder.

Caffe Frost:

2 tsps. sugar
2 cups hot strong coffee
1/4 cup Sambuca Romana
Dissolve sugar into coffee. Cool. Pour into ice cube tray and freeze.
Crush coffee cubes and then combine in blender with Sambuca
Romana. Blend until sherbety. Spoon into chilled sherbet glasses.
4 servings.

PERNOD

In the XVIIth century, Henri Louis Pernod introduced this drink made of a blend of seventeen herbs and plants including anise, to France. The time was particularly well-chosen: the XVIIth century coffee houses had become cafés and served lemonade, colorful spirits and the opalescent yellow-greenish Pernod along with coffee just as they do now. It has been rumored but not proven that Toulouse-Lautrec had a walking stick with a built-in flask for Pernod. Many years later Ernest Hemingway who was an habitué of the Paris cafés sang the praises of Pernod in "For Whom The Bell Tolls".

DRINKS

Here is the French way to drink Pernod:
5 to 6 parts of water for one part Pernod over ice.
It is drunk in France before dinner as "an apéritif". It also blends very well with grapefruit, orange, pineapple and cranberry juice, or try a:

Sunset

2 oz. Pernod
1/2 oz. grenadine
Chilled water, ice cubes
Place ice cubes in an 8 oz. glass. Add Pernod and Grenadine.
Fill the glass with chilled water and stir.

ENTREES

Pernod adds to the finesse of fish and shell fish; the anise flavor blends very well with the herbs and spices traditionally used in preparing fish: chervil, chives, thyme, bay leaves, parsley, cloves, fennel and saffron.

MOULES MARINIERE

5 pints mussels
1/2 pint water
6 sprigs parsley
a pinch of thyme
1 finely sliced onion
1/2 bay leaf
2 tbsps. Pernod

Sauce
1 cup white wine (dry)
1 small chopped shallot
1 tbsp. chopped parsley
3 oz. butter

Scrub mussels carefully to remove all sand and grit. Place them with the ingredients mentioned above — except the Pernod in a large saucepan with a tight fitting lid. Place the saucepan on high flame (gas) or high heat (electric); after 2 minutes shake the covered saucepan, continue shaking every minute until the mussels are cooked. When all the mussels have opened, they are ready (discard any mussel that has remained closed). Remove mussels from saucepan; keep them in a warm place until the sauce is ready.

Sauce: Put wine and shallots in a large saucepan. Cook rapidly until wine is reduced to half its quantity. Add liquid from the mussels and the Pernod. Bring to a boil, add butter cut in tiny pieces, mix well, add parsley. Add the mussels, warm on the stove for a few minutes and serve. Serves 6.

Add a dash of Pernod to your favorite fish soup.

FILETS OF FLOUNDER OR SOLE WITH PERNOD

Preheat oven to 350°
4 large filets of sole or flounder
Salt and pepper (to taste)
The juice of a lemon
1 tsp. thyme
2 tbsps. chopped parsley
1 cup white wine (or ½ cup white wine, ½ cup clam juice)
2 tbsps. Pernod

Put the filets of sole in a large shallow baking pan. Sprinkle with salt, pepper, lemon juice, dried thyme and parsley. Pour the white wine over the fish. Put in the oven. After 15 minutes, add the Pernod. Return to oven. Fish is done when it flakes easily (about 30-35 minutes). Serves 4.

For a richer sauce (and more calories) dot the fish with butter before putting it in the oven.

162

Spicy Beef Anisette

163

Iced Potage Senegalese

164

AFTER DINNER DRINKS

Put 1 or 2 teaspoons Pernod in your cup of espresso coffee.

HERBSAINT

(An anise flavored liqueur popular in Louisiana)

If you find yourself in New-Orleans, order it, especially if you are suffering from a hangover.

2 oz. Herbsaint
1 egg white
1 teaspoon anisette
1 teaspoon Orgeat (almond syrup)
Club soda if wanted
Crushed ice
Shake well.

This same recipe made with Pernod was said to be one of Toulouse Lautrec's favorite drinks.

MORE ABOUT ANISE

FRANCE.   **Amourette:**   an absinthe substitute for perfect lovers.
Pastis: This cousin of Pernod is the traditional aperitif of Southern France.

GREECE.   **Ouzo and Mastic:**   more fiery, less sweet than anisette. They are generally drunk on the rocks.

ITALY.   **Anesone:**   higher in proof and drier than anisette. In need of warmth? Try the "White Heat":

        $1/2$ oz. Stock Anesone
        $1\frac{1}{2}$ oz. of vodka

Pour over ice cubes in an old-fashioned glass.

PORTUGAL.   **Beirao:**   a tasty combination of orange and anise.

SPAIN.   **Anise del Mono** and **Ojen.** Anise liqueurs are as popular in Spain as scotch and gin in the United States. They are generally drunk on the rocks.

TURKEY.   **Raki:**   a generic name for all liqueurs with aniseed and licorice flavors. These liqueurs are stronger than Anisette and widely appreciated in the Near East.

A Taste of Caraway

KUMMEL

It is such a great "Northern" liqueur that to claim its origin is an honor sought by many. The old firm of Bols in Holland says that their Bolskümmel, first distilled in 1575, is the original one. The Germans claim also that they invented kümmel. Whatever its creator, Gilka kümmel, made in Germany has been considered the standard quality kummel for almost a century.

The recipe from Holland was brought back to Russia by Peter the Great at the turn of the XVIIIth century. It quickly became immensely popular at the court of the Czars and to this day it can be considered a Russian and a Polish favorite.

There are two types of kümmel; the drier is the white or Allasch type which has become a generic name. Allasch is named after an estate in Latvia, near Riga, famous for the excellence of its cumin and caraway seeds. The black or Eckau, a Russian type kümmel, is a bit heavier and sweeter. A kümmel liqueur is made with caraway, cumin and sometimes coriander seeds mixed with a distillation of barley, wheat or corn.

The caraway plant is grown mainly for its highly flavored seed. Related to the carrot family, it was known in the ancient world and used for its many medicinal qualities. For instance, it was used to bring down fever. Jewish and European cooks make a greater use of the seed than the British and American ones. In Germany and Austria, it is often added to bread, a practice that is spreading in the United Kingdom and in the United States. In Alsace, they serve a delightful snack: Munster cheese sprinkled with caraway seeds. Try it, it's delicious!

Cumin is a plant similar to rue and parsley, but it tastes like caraway. It was known to ancient civilizations. It is mentioned in the Bible (Isaiah 28:25 and 27) where the prophet insists that God takes care of the smallest seeds, even cumin seeds. It originated in Egypt and was known through the centuries as a carminative and as an antispasmodic; a remedy against indigestion, headaches or gout. Nowadays it is used as a spice to flavor bread and to make kummel.

Coriander is a parsley-like plant which originated in the eastern Mediterranean region. Its medicinal properties have been known for centuries and resemble those of cumin and caraway. But in Mediterranean countries, the leaves are used as a pot-herb. They are known to clear the complexion and are said to be an aphrodisiac. Coriander seeds, crushed and burned were used as a base for a hallucinogen introduced into China by the Scythians and from then on in Chinese legends, coriander conferred immortality. Coriander seeds are often found as an ingredient in curry powder along with tumeric, ginger, cayenne pepper, and other spices.

DRINKS

Kümmel has a very special taste, so distinctive that you will either love it or hate it.

It is usually served straight but it is also quite enjoyable with vodka or gin:
4 parts vodka
1 part kümmel
Serve on the rocks

A different martini:
3/4 oz. kümmel
3/4 oz. gin
2 dashes very dry vermouth
Strain over crushed ice

168

ENTREES

CORDIAL CHICKEN KIEV

3/4 cup unsifted, all-purpose
  flour
3 eggs well beaten
1 1/2 cup packaged dry bread
crumbs (or you can make your
  own)
Salad oil or shortening for
deep frying
6 boned and skinned whole
  chicken breasts
They are available in that form
in supermarkets, or you can ask
your butcher to bone and skin
them for you, and save the
bones to flavor soups.

Herb Butter
1 cup butter or margarine,
  softened
2 tbsps. chopped parsley
1 1/2 tsps. dried tarragon
  leaves (or chopped fresh
  leaves if available)
1 clove garlic, crushed
3/4 tsp. salt
1/8 tsp. freshly ground pepper
1 tbsp. kümmel

First prepare the herb butter; in a small bowl mix all the ingredients. On foil paper, shape into a 6 in. square. Wrap foil around the butter and freeze for about 40 minutes.

Meanwhile wash chicken and flatten it with a mallet. Be careful not to break the meat. Cut frozen butter into 12 parts. Place a pat of herb butter in center of each piece of chicken, fold chicken over the butter and fasten with toothpick, be careful that no butter is showing. Roll chicken in flour on wax paper, dip each piece in beaten eggs and coat with breadcrumbs. Refrigerate, covered until chilled (about 1 hour). In a heavy saucepan, slowly heat oil (it should be about 3 inches deep) to 360°. Add chicken 3 pieces at a time, fry turning with tongs till browned (about 5 minutes). Drain on paper towels. Keep warm in 200° oven in a large pan lined with paper towels, but not more than 15 minutes so that the chicken does not dry. Serves 6.

Chicken Kiev can be made in advance and frozen.
To serve, do not defrost. Bake uncovered for 35 minutes in 350° oven.

Herb butter is also delicious over a sizzling steak.

Deep frying oil can be reused two or three times: strain to remove bits of bread crumbs or meat, store in refrigerator in a tightly covered jar.

KUMMEL SALAD DRESSING

for 1 cup dressing
3/4 cup salad oil
1/4 cup vinegar (or lemon juice)
1 tbsp. mustard
1 tbsp. ricotta cheese or heavy
   cream
1 good dash of kümmel

Mix mustard and vinegar, add oil and beat until smooth, add ricotta or cream, kümmel and mix well.

Delicious over green salad, or any type of mixed salad (lettuce, tomatoes, cucumber, avocados), also on a chef salad.

CHEESE FONDUE,
(Eastern European Fashion)

1½ grated Gruyère cheese
2 cups dry white wine
2 tps. cornflour
4 tbsps. kümmel
1 clove garlic
Nutmeg, pepper
French bread cut in small pieces

Rub the inside of a chafing dish or other suitable pan with garlic. Heat the wine in it, then add the cheese, stirring constantly. As soon as the cheese bubbles, add the cornflour blended with the kümmel. Season with pepper to taste and grated nutmeg. Keep the fondue hot and bubbling on small spirit stove, unless you own an electric fondue pot. Spear pieces of bread on long forks and dip into the bubbling cheese. Enjoy it.

Add a dash of kümmel to your favorite curry dish.

Kümmel does not lend itself to desserts.

AFTER DINNER DRINKS

On the rocks, or with vodka and gin (see drinks at the beginning of this section).

DANZIGER GOLDWASSER

This liqueur originated in Danzig. In the best tradition of the alchemists it was water white. It was flavored with caraway and anise seeds. In the Middle Ages gold flakes were added to the liqueur because it was then a common belief that gold in any form improved the human body. This final trick of opulence also marked the wealth of Old Danzig in Prussia which became the Polish city of Dansk.

This belief in the power of gold was shared by the maharajas from India. In their palaces, sweets were served, sprinkled with gold dust, to honor the guest and help the digestion.

Gold water is sold in France under the name of Liqueur d'or. Italy provides another type of gold water or Acqua d'oro: oil of cinnamon, coriander, lemon, mace and orange blossoms in neutral spirit, with sugar and gold flecks. It was introduced in France by Catherine de Medicis. There is another Italian variation made of fruit peels, licorice, rosemary flowers and gold flakes. If you add the virtues of gold to the effect of rosemary, which is not only a symbol of fidelity and remembrance, but also a stimulant of brain and memory, this must indeed be a remarkable liqueur.

Landing a Large Party....Punches and Hors d'oeuvres

The ingredients can be doubled or tripled to make a larger quantity.

EGGNOG LUCULLUS

4 eggs, separated
Pinch of salt
1 tbsp. sugar
8 oz. Sambuca Romana
4 oz. bourbon
1½ cups milk
1/2 pint heavy cream, whipped

Beat egg whites stiff with salt. In another bowl, beat egg yolks with sugar until thick. Gradually beat in Sambuca Romana, bourbon and milk. Gently fold in beaten egg whites, then whipped cream. Dust with nutmeg. Serves 12.

Or you can make a very nourishing eggnog by using as a base **Advocaat,** a rich, sweet thick cordial from Holland, made of egg yolks, sugar and neutral spirits.

To revive your spirits after trudging in the snow, add to one bottle of Advocaat:

16 oz. brandy or cognac
1 qt. of milk
1 pt. heavy cream

You can serve this punch iced or hot. Serves about 20.

173

APRICOT SOUR PUNCH

1 qt. blended whisky
8 oz. apricot flavored brandy
juice of one lemon
1 cup apricot halves
1 cup strawberries
club soda

In a large punch bowl pour over block of ice 1 quart blended whisky, 8 oz. apricot flavored brandy and the juice of one lemon. Stir well. Garnish with apricot halves and strawberry. Just before serving add a splash of soda water. Serves 12.

CASSIS PUNCH

16 oz. crème de cassis
16 oz. rum (dark or light)
6 lemons
1 quart soda water

Put block of ice in punch bowl. Pour in crème de cassis and rum. Mix well. Add the sliced lemons. Just before serving, add soda water. Serves 15.

COINTREAU PUNCH

2 qts. frozen orange juice
1½ qts. frozen pineapple juice
1 qt. Cointreau
1 quart white rum
1 pt. grenadine

Mix all the ingredients in a large punch bowl. If you want a decorative touch, freeze fruit in a jello mold and let it float in punch instead of block of ice. Serves 20 to 30.

CHAMPAGNE PUNCH

1½ cups sugar
2 cups freshly squeezed lemon
  juice
3 bottles dry champagne
  (chilled)
1 cup Cointreau
1 lemon, unpeeled, slice thin
  into cartwheels
Fresh strawberries

Stir sugar into lemon juice until it dissolves. Chill thoroughly just before serving over a block of ice in punch bowl. Gently stir the champagne, add Cointreau. Garnish with lemon cartwheels and sliced strawberries. Serves 20.

BELLY DANCER PUNCH

24 parts milk
24 parts Régnier Pistàshà

Pour over ice, stir well and add grated nutmeg on top of each glass. Serves 24.

CRANBERRY PUNCH

1/4 cup superfine sugar
2 cups fresh lemon juice
1 quart light rum
1 quart cold water
3 oz. Boggs cranberry liqueur
Block of ice
1 quart cognac
1 cup sliced, peeled, fresh,
   frozen or canned fruit

Put in punch bowl and stir with a muddler to dissolve the sugar thoroughly. Add the rum, water, Boggs cranberry liqueur and cognac. Stir and allow the punch to set at room temperature for 2 hours stirring occasionally. Put the block of ice into the bowl and garnish with fruit, if desired. Serve in punch cups. Serves 24.

RHINE WINE PUNCH

5 cups fresh fruits — choose
   your favorite but include
   peeled oranges and sliced
   lemons
20 maraschino cherries
20 oz. brandy
20 oz. Bénédictine
20 oz. maraschino liqueur
5 bottles chilled Rhine wine
32 oz. chilled club soda
A block of ice

Place fruits in the punch bowl first, add cherries and brandy, Bénédictine and maraschino liqueur. Put the bowl in the freezer for ½ hour. Remove and add block of ice. Just before serving add the Rhine wine and club soda. Stir and serve. Serve 20.

PEACH FLAVORED RUM PUNCH

8 oz. superfine sugar
24 oz. lime juice (fresh squeezed
   if possible)
2 qts. light rum
1 qt. dark rum
8 oz. peach flavored brandy.

In a large punch bowl, mix the ingredients. Stir well and chill for at least two hours. Before serving, add a block of ice. Serve 20 to 30.

If you do not own a punch bowl, don't let it stop you. They can be rented quite easily.

HORS D'OEUVRES

To serve with punches or to complement a cocktail hour or when you are not in the mood to fix a real dinner:

PISTASHA MEAT BALLS

1 lb. ground beef
1 lb. ground lamb
1 onion, grated
1/2 teaspoon salt
1 teaspoon oregano
1 teaspoon basil
1/2 teaspoon cumin seed
1 tablespoon chopped parsley
  (finely)
5 oz. chopped pistachio nuts
1/2 teaspoon coriander seed
1/4 cup Régnier Pistàshà
2 eggs
4 oz. Pepperidge Farm Herb
  Stuffing
1/2 cup water

Mix above ingredients; with your hands, lightly shape into 1″ diameter meatballs. In 1 — 2 oz. of hot oil in large skillet, brown meatballs all over, remove as they are brown. Arrange meatballs in heated dish and spoon sauce around.

Sauce
6 tablespoons butter
1 medium onion grated
2 medium apples grated
3 tablespoons flour
2 tablespoons curry powder
1½ cups beef broth
3 oz. Pistàshà

Melt butter in skillet, add onion and apple, and cook until tender, not browned. Stir in broth, bring to a boil, and simmer until sauce is thickened. Add Pistàshà. Dip meatballs in sauce or pour over meatballs.

SPARERIBS

4 lbs. spareribs
3 tbsps. Sambuca Romana
1/4 cup soy sauce
2 tbsps. vinegar
2 garlic cloves, crushed
1/4 tsp. each ginger and
  pepper

Cut spareribs apart and marinate in remaining ingredients. Arrange ribs in shallow foil-lined pan. Bake in pre-heated 375⁰ oven 1¼ hours, turning occasionally and basting with marinade. Serves 6-8.

CHEESE NUGGETS

1/2 lb. blue cheese
1/2 lb. cream cheese
1/4 cup Sambuca Romana
1 cup finely chopped nuts

Whip cheeses with Sambuca Romana. Chill. Shape into 1-inch balls. Roll in nuts. Chill. About 4 dozen.

WATERMELON BASKET

Fill hollowed watermelon shell with variety of cut fresh summer fruits and berries. Add 4 oz. Amaretto di Saronno to each 1½ qts. of fruit. Serve chilled.

POLYNESIAN DIPPING SAUCE

1 jar (9 oz.) chutney
1/2 Boggs cranberry
  liqueur
1/4 cup water

Place all ingredients in blender and blend until smooth. Pour into 2 qt. saucepan. Simmer 5 minutes or until desired consistency. Serve with hot fried shrimp or fish and Chinese egg rolls. Makes about 2 cups sauce.

DIP FOR FRESH VEGETABLES

2 pints sour cream
2 packages dehydrated onion
  soup mix
1 cup walnuts sliced thin
1 cup anisette

Mix well and chill covered for at least two hours. Serve with celery and carrot sticks, sliced zucchinis and cauliflower buds.

COCKTAIL SHISH-KEBABS

20 small mushrooms, washed
  and wiped dry
1 package (12 ounces) cocktail
  franks
1/3 cup butter
1/3 cup kümmel

Saute mushrooms and franks in butter and kümmel over medium flame (10 minutes). Spear mushrooms and franks on toothpicks.

CHEESE SPREAD

1 lb. grated Edam or cheddar
  cheese
1/4 cup soft butter or margarine
1 tsp. dry mustard
1/2 tsp. Worcestershire sauce
Dash of Tabasco
3 tbsps. cherry flavored brandy

Mix all ingredients in a bowl. Chill overnight. Serve with crackers or celery stalks.

MEAD PATE

1 lb. liverwurst
1/2 cup butter or margarine
  (softened)
1/4 cup Irish Mist
1 can (3¼ oz.) pitted ripe
  olives (sliced)
Freshly ground pepper to taste

Mash liverwurst and butter together thoroughly. Blend in remaining ingredients. Pack into a mold. Chill. When ready to serve, unmold and garnish with red pepper strips and parsley. Serve with buttered toasted French bread slices or with crackers.

DEVILED EGGS

Cut cold hard-boiled eggs in half. Remove yolks. Blend with mayonnaise, salt, pepper and paprika to taste. Add 1 tbsp. ginger flavored brandy per 4 eggs. Spoon mixture back into eggs. Sprinkle with paprika and serve cold.

HELPFUL SUGGESTIONS

Go back to our recipe for chicken livers Kalhúa. Proceed according to recipe. Then put the cooked mixture in a blender until pureed. Chill and serve as a pate with toasted French bread or crackers.

A large ham glazed with orange liqueur, apricot or peach flavored brandy   can be made in advance, sliced and served with French bread, melba toast or cracker.

CONCLUSION

LIQUEURS MENTIONED
IN THE TEXT

*There are no drink recipes for the liqueurs preceded with an asterisk.

Advocaat 173
Amaretto di Saronno 93
*Amourette 166
Anesone 166
*Angel Elixir 56
*Angelica Cordial 56
Anis del mono 166
Anisette 147
Apricot flavored brandy 124
*Aqua Turco 72
Aurum 118

*Bahia 84
*Banana Nectar 141
*Beirao 166
Bénédictine 47
B & B 52
Blackberry flavored brandy 134

*Calisay 56
*Centerbe 56
Chartreuse 37
*Cherry Bestle 141
*Cherry flavored brandy 141
Cheri-Suisse 89
Choclair 90
Chocolate Almond 102
*Chocolate-Amaretto 91
*Chocolate-Banana 91
*Chocolate-Orange 91

GUIDE TO RECIPES IN THE TEXT

Entrees

MEATS

BEEF

LAMB

PORK

HAM

Baked Ham Romana (sambuca-Romana) 158
Barbecued Ham steaks (Tia Maria) 81
Baked Fresh Ham Chartreuse (Chartreuse) 41

VEAL

Veal à l'Orange Reina (amaretto-di Saronno) 95
Escalopes de veau (apricot flavored brandy-Régnier) 125
Veal Scallopini (curaçao-Arrow) 107

POULTRY

CHICKEN

Barbecued chicken Bénédictine (Bénédictine) 48
Flamingo stuffed chicken (curaçao-Arrow) 106
Chicken Suprême (Chartreuse) 41
Chicken breasts apricot (apricot flavored brandy) 124
Cordial chicken Kiev (kümmel) 169
Ole chicken Mole (crème de cacao) 86
Pollo Venetto (sambuca-Romana) 157
Chicken livers
Chicken livers Kalhúa (Kalhúa) 76
Chicken livers with an oriental taste (ginger flavored brandy) 74

CORNISH HENS

Rock cornish hens (crème de cassis-Régnier) 139

DUCK

Duckling à l'orange (Cointreau) 114

TURKEY

Roast Turkey with cranberry sauce (cranberry liqueur-Boggs) 129

FISH AND SHELL FISH

Filets of sole or flounder (Pernod) 162
Lobster in cucumber boats (anisette-Marie Brizard) 149
Moules Marinière (Pernod) 162
Shrimp Capri (sambuca-Romana) 157
Sauteed shrimp with Chartreuse (Chartreuse) 40
Shrimp dip (Tia Maria) 81
Sole au gratin (Cointreau) 113

SOUPS

Beef-barley soup (Irish Mist) 61
Iced Potage Senegalese (anisette-Marie Brizard) 148
Jamaican Asparagus soup (Tia Maria) 80
Mushroom soup (B & B) 52

Sweet soups
Apple soup (Peter Heering) 121
Cherry soup cassis (crème de cassis) 139
Dessert fruit soup (cranberry liqueur-Boggs) 132
Rubarb soup (Peter Heering) 122

VEGETABLES AND SIDE DISHES

Artichokes vinaigrette (crème de menthe) 70
Baked acorn squash (Irish Mist) 62
Carrots del Turco (amaretto-di Saronno) 96
Carrot Purée (anisette-Marie Brizard) 149
Cranberry candied yams (cranberry liqueur-Boggs) 130
Rizotto au Cointreau (Cointreau) 114
Rosy-red beets (cranberry liqueur-Boggs) 131

SAUCES AND RELISH

Barbecue Sauce (Galliano) 57
Boggs cranberry sauce (cranberry-Boggs) 129
Peach conserve (amaretto-di Saronno) 94
Spicy sauce for boiled beef or left over pot-roast (blackberry-flavored brandy) 135
Spicy cranberry sauce (amaretto-di Saronno) 95

Sweet sauces

Sambuca sauce (sambuca-Romana) 159

Fresh fruit topping (crème de menthe and crème de cacao) 71

FONDUE

Cheese fondue (kümmel) 170

COFFEE

Amaretto and coffee (amaretto-di Saronno) 101

Cafe Bénédictine (Bénédictine) 51

Café B & B (B&B) 53

Café Diable (Cointreau) 116

Café et Pernod (Pernod) 165

Espresso and anisette (anisette-Marie Brizard) 151

French coffee (Cointreau) 117

Irish Mist coffee (Irish Mist) 64

Jamaican coffee (Tia Maria) 83

Mexican coffee (crème de cacao) 88

Mocha coffee (Cointreau) 117

Romana coffee (sambuca-Romana) 160

Sweet Volcano (Kalhúa) 78

PUNCHES

Belly dancer punch (Pistàshà liqueur-Régnier) 174.

Cassis punch (crème de cassis) 174

Champagne punch (Cointreau) 174

Cointreau punch (Cointreau) 174

Cranberry punch (cranberry liqueur-Boggs) 175

Eggnog Advocaat (Advocaat liqueur) 173

Eggnog Luculllus (Sambuca-Romana) 173

Peach flavored rum punch (peach flavored brandy) 175

Rhine Wine punch (Bénédictine and maraschino liqueur) 175

HORS D'OEUVRES

Cheese nuggets (sambuca-Romana) 177

Cheese spread (cherry flavored brandy) 178

Chicken livers pate (Kalhúa) 76

Cocktail shish-kebabs (kümmel) 178

Dip for fresh vegetables (anisette) 178
Mead pate (Irish Mist) 179
Pistasha meatballs (Pistàshà liqueur-Régnier) 176
Polynesian dipping sauce (cranberry liqueur-Boggs) 177
Spareribs Sambuca (sambuca-Romana) 177
Water melon basket (amaretto-di Saronno) 177

DESSERTS

CAKES AND PIES

Chiffon Pie (Izarra) 55
Coffee Anisette cake (anisette-Marie Brizard) 151
Cranberria Vacherin (Cranberria-Régnier) 133
Cranberry Peach Melba (cranberry liqueur-Boggs) 131
Creme de cacao cake (crème de cacao) 87
Grasshopper Pie (crème de menthe-crème de cacao) 87
Mocha Cheese Cake (amaretto-di Saronno) 101
Mocha Sponge Cake (Bénédictine) 51
Pie suprise (Tia Maria) 82

COLD DESERTS

Appricot Alaska (apricot flavored brandy) 126
Biscottini (sambuca-Romana) 159
Cassis rainbow (crème de cassis) 140
Chartreuse Bavarian cream with strawberries (Chartreuse) 43
Dutch Mint (crème de menthe) 70
Jello a la Sambuca (sambuca-Romana) 158
Kalhúa ice-cream (Kalhúa) 78
Quick crème de menthe frappé (crème de menthe) 70
Stars and stripes (crème de menthe-crème de cacao) 71
Valhalla (Irish Mist) 64

FLAMBES DESSERTS

Banana-pineapple flambe (Irish Mist) 63
Chaud et froid (Cointreau) 117
Cheri-jubilee (Cheri-Suisse) 90
Crêpes flambées (Cointreau) 115

Omelette flambée (curaçao) 107
Peach Jubilee (sambuca-Romana) 158

FRUIT DESSERTS

Cinnamon apples (Irish Mist) 63
Cranberry Peach Melba (cranberry Liquer-Boggs) 131
Creamy fruit dessert (Choclair) 90
Cuban bananas (blackberry flavored brandy) 136
Fresh strawberries a la Amaretto (amaretto-di Saronno) 97
Fresh strawberries with Peter Heering (Peter Heering) 122
Frosty fruit compote (cranberry liqueur-Boggs) 132
Fruit compote Anisette (anisette-Marie Brizard) 150
Fruit in Cointreau syrup (Cointreau) 116
Fruits minceur (Cointreau) 116
Fruit salad cassis (crème de cassis) 140
Peach cassis (crème de cassis) 140
Poires cacao (crème de cacao) 88

MOUSSES

Apricot mousse (apricot flavored brandy) 126
Kalhúa mousse (Kalhúa) 77
Mousse au chocolat with French cream (anisette-Marie Brizard) 150
Pumpkin mousse (amaretto-di Saronno) 99

SOUFFLES OR SOUFFLES LIKE DESSERTS

Neige à la Chartreuse (Chartreuse) 42
Citron Chartreuse Soufflé (Chartreuse) 44

MISCELLANEOUS

Amaretto zabaglione (amaretto-di Saronno) 98
Banana Split, Italian style (amaretto-di Saronno) 99
Chocolate fondue (amaretto-di Saronno) 98

SELECTED BIBLIOGRAPHY

Ars Distillandi, Brunswich 1512.

BROTHWELL, Don & Patricia. *Food in Antiquity. A Survey of the Diet of Early People*. London, 1969.

CULPEPER, N. *The English Physician*. Numerous editions.

HALLGARTEN, Peter. *Liqueurs*. London, 1967.

HANNUM & BLUMBERG. *Brandies and liqueurs of the World*. New York, 1976.

HIBBERT, Christofer. *The House of Medici: its rise and fall*. New York, 1975.

HOWE, S. E. *In Quest of Spices*. London, 1946.

HUYSMANS, J. - K. *A Rebours*. Paris, 1884.
                          Against Nature. Penguin Books, 1976.
                          Translated by Robert Baldick.

KRAMER, Samuel Noah, *L'Histoire commence à Sumer*. Paris, 1957.

LEYEL, C. F. *The Magic of Herbs*. London, 1926.

MARCO POLO. *La description du monde*. Paris, 1955.

RAY, Cyril. *The Complete book of Spirits and Liqueurs*. New York, 1978.

RUDENKO, Sergei. *Frozen Tombs of Siberia; The Pazyryk Burials of Iron Age Horsemen* (Tr. M.W. Thompsen), Univ. Of Cal. Press, Berkeley, 1970.

VILLANOVA, Alnardus de. *The earliest Printed Book on Wine by A. de V. Physician, Surgon, Botanist, Alchemist and Philosopher*. [1235-1311], Schuman, New York, 1943.

VRIES, Ad. de. *Dictionary of Symbols and Imagery*. Amsterdam, 1974.

YOUNGER, William. *Gods, Men and Wine*. London, 1966.

We wish to thank the Cordial Houses and their representatives who gave us permission to reprint recipes. The names of the various liqueurs appear throughout the text in their respective recipes.

Acknowledgement for Illustrations

AMARETTO DI SARONNO (Foreign Vintages, N.Y.) pp. 92, 100.

BENEDICTINE (Julius Wile Sons & Co., N.Y.), p.46.

CHARTREUSE (Schieffelin & Co., N.Y.) pp. 5, 6, 8, 19, 20, 39, 45, 50.

COINTREAU (Cointreau USA), pp.109, 110.

MARIE BRIZARD ANISETTE (Schieffelin & Co.), pp.146, 163, 164.

IRISH MIST (Heublein), pp. 21.

A Personal Touch

Having brought yourself and your guests into the magic circle of sophistication, culture, and exotism, *create* your own adventures in the world of liqueurs. Record your favorite liqueur recipes, comments and guests' suggestions, the highlights of your experiences.

Date: Food or beverage served:

Date: Food or beverage served: